THE Colorado Weather BOOK

TEXT BY
Mike Nelson
and the **9NEWS** Weather Team

FOREWORD BY
Ed Sardella

WESTCLIFFE PUBLISHERS

ENGLEWOOD, COLORADO

For my Dad,

whose inspiration

and enthusiasm

live on in me.

Table of Contents

ISBN: 1-56579-342-0

Text Copyright: Mike Nelson, 1999
All rights reserved

Illustration Copyright: Jonathan Moreno, 1999
All rights reserved

Photography Copyright: see page 133

Editor: Kristen Iversen

Production Manager: Craig Keyzer

Editorial Assistant: Anne Lanctot

Research Assistant: Joyanna Laughlin

Design Concept: Rebecca Finkel,
F + P Graphic Design, Boulder, CO

Published by: Westcliffe Publishers, Inc.
P.O. Box 1261
Englewood, CO 80150
www.westcliffepublishers.com

Printed in: Hong Kong

Printed by: C & C Offset Printing Co., Ltd.

**Library of Congress
Cataloging-In-Publication Data**

Nelson, Mike P., 1957–

The Colorado weather book / by Mike
Nelson and the 9NEWS weather team.

p.   cm.

Includes Index.

ISBN 1-56579-342-0

1. Colorado—Climate. 2. Weather.
I. Title.

QC984.C7N45 1999   99-17298
551.69788—dc21   CIP

*For more information about other fine
books and calendars from Westcliffe
Publishers, please call your local bookstore, contact us
at 1-800-523-3692, write for our free
color catalog, or visit us on the web at
www.westcliffepublishers.com.*

Acknowledgments

To put this into weatherman terms, the probability of my writing a book might have been "less than twenty percent." Not that I didn't think about it over the years, but the thought was seldom more than fleeting. Like most of us, the daily tasks of living, working, and raising kids seemed more than enough. So when the folks at Westcliffe Publishers as well as Roger Ogden and Patti Dennis at 9NEWS approached me with the idea, I felt a little overwhelmed at first. Beginning a project such as this is like standing at the foot of a very tall mountain with the prospect of a long climb ahead. Fortunately, I have been aided in that climb by the help of some wonderful people.

First of all, I wish to thank my wonderful children, Anders and Christiana. They are the warmth and sunshine of my life. I am grateful to my parents, Arliss and John, who instilled so many values in me—some that I am discovering even to this day. I love you, Mom; I miss you, Dad. Thanks to my sisters, Nancy and Kristin, for providing help with getting me through those awkward first forty years.

From a professional standpoint, thanks to my colleagues in the 9NEWS Weather Center: Ed Greene, Kathy Sabine, and Nick Carter. They're a terrific trio to work with and appear in this book many times. Kudos to Andy Schaeffer and Pam Berube for their help with some of the 9NEWS photos. Also, thanks to Roger Ogden and Patti Dennis for their support and encouragement.

Over the longer term, I must acknowledge some people who helped guide my journey into and through meteorology. Two of the legends of television weather provided great inspiration: Harry Volkman from Chicago, who always had a flower in his lapel from the grade school he visited that day; and the late Stormy Rottman, the Denver weatherman, who remains my personal hero. I'm grateful to two people from the University of Wisconsin: Dr. Frank Sechrist, who showed me around the Meteorology Department when I was about fourteen years old and later became my synoptic professor; and the late Dr. Lyle Horn, my major professor at the University of Wisconsin who was one of the kindest men I have ever known. I also want to thank Tom Skilling, the weatherman at WGN-TV in Chicago. I watched Tom at his first television job on WKOW-TV in Madison. Tom's enthusiasm for weather touched off an early flame in me.

There is one person that I can truly call my mentor. I cannot thank Terry Kelly enough for all that he has done to help me get where I am today. Terry hired me as a college freshman and we worked together for nearly a decade. No one has taught me more about television weather than Terry Kelly.

A special thanks to the great people at Westcliffe for all of their guidance, especially Kristen Iversen, who worked with me every step of the way. Craig Keyzer's enthusiasm and expertise show on every page. It is a great thrill to be within the same pages as John Fielder, whom I have long admired and respected. And special thanks to Joyanna Laughlin, our researcher. Joyanna provided many of the interview segments in the book and her name reflects the happy experience of working with her.

There are many excellent weather resource people along the Front Range. Thank you to the folks in Boulder: Bob Henson, Kevin Trenberth, Michael Glantz, and John Snook. Their information on El Niño, climate change, and other cutting-edge research was invaluable. Also, thanks to Nolan Doesken at the Colorado Climate Center. Nolan is not just a very nice person; he knows more about the history of Colorado weather than anyone else.

I'd like to acknowledge all of the contributors to this book, who appear in various sidebars and add much flavor to the text. Also, kudos to two former interns, Randy Brock and Wayne Tybon, for their work in gathering weather web sites.

Finally, words cannot express the love and gratitude I feel for Cindy, my wife and soul mate. It is fitting that my first book is about Colorado. Although neither of us was lucky enough to be born here, we both feel that we are "native in spirit." The two decades we have spent together have been a fabulous ride that has fortunately found us in this beautiful state. Cindy has taught me many things, but the most important is that the secret of life is enjoying the passage of time.

— MIKE NELSON

Foreword

We who do the *news* part of the 9NEWS broadcast hate to admit it, but we know the weather report is one of the most important reasons—if not *the* most important reason—that you watch the local news. We know many of you watch 9NEWS at 10:00 P.M. to find out the next day's weather so that you can plan your day. (Some of you go to bed as soon as the weather's over. No offense, Ron Zappolo!)

If weather's that important to you, then it's that important to us, too. We take weather very seriously, and we make sure our weather team really knows its stuff. This book proves it.

When television stations choose their weather reporters, some of them choose a good performer who has picked up some weather knowledge here and there. Or they pick a weather specialist who can perform adequately on the air. At 9NEWS, our weather reporters are highly skilled at both, contributing to a rich history that goes back to our pioneering weatherman, Stormy Rottman.

Mike Nelson and his cohorts in the 9NEWS weather station have been good enough to share some of their expertise on Colorado's weather in written form so that you can have it at your fingertips. This book will help you understand the terms and symbols they use, and it will give you insight into how they arrive at their predictions. Maybe the book will help you make a pretty fair prediction, occasionally, yourself. Notice I said "occasionally." Don't get overconfident and decide you can forecast the weather by yourself. We need you as a 9NEWS viewer. And besides, you might leave your coat at home on a day it snows! Now's the time to snicker and say, "We sometimes do that anyway, because of what those weather people say on the news." We love to give them a hard time, don't we?

Forecasting the weather is a complex science. Reporting on the weather in Colorado is an even greater challenge. This book tells us why it's so much harder here, and Mike has written it in language that all of us can understand. When you finish reading *The Colorado Weather Book,* I promise you'll have even greater respect for the skill and knowledge of our 9NEWS weather team. I certainly do. Thanks to Mike and the team for sharing.   .

Bright and sunny days to all of you from all of us at 9NEWS.

— ED SARDELLA

Colorado SPRING

Heavy snows in the mountains, severe storms on the plains, and sunshine in Denver—often at the same time! That's springtime in the Rockies. Spring is the most volatile season in Colorado as the cold air of winter grudgingly makes way for the increasing warmth of the new season. The calendar is meaningless in spring—the third week of March means little to the atmosphere over our state. Surrounding states to the south and east may

be enjoying the first green shoots of the leaves and the bright yellow flowers of daffodils, but in Colorado we still have plenty of fickle weather to contend with.

The beginning of spring can also bring the biggest snowstorms of the year. In fact, the record for the most snow in a 24-hour period was set on April 14–15, 1921, at Silver Lake in Boulder County when a storm brought 76 inches. This record was unbeaten until a town in New York State allegedly claimed a higher snowfall by two-tenths of an inch a few years ago—although some Colorado climate historians don't believe it!

Why does Colorado experience such big snowstorms in the springtime? As temperatures begin to warm over the Gulf of Mexico, moist air moves off the waters of the Gulf and begins to head north with more vigor. The severe weather season is kicked into high gear over Texas and Oklahoma, but in Colorado our temperatures are still chilly due to the combination of higher latitude and altitude. Moist Gulf air clashes with the stubborn cold of the past season and creates big storm systems. Several factors combine to produce these powerful storms: the growing warmth from the south,

DAYS OF SPRING

■ FRONT RANGE
based on Denver

	March	April	May
Average Normal High	52°	62°	71°
Average Normal Low	26°	35°	44°
Record High	84°	90°	95°
Record Low	–11°	–2°	19°
Average Precipitation	1.3"	1.7"	2.6"

■ HIGH COUNTRY
based on Aspen

	March	April	May
Average Normal High	43°	53°	64°
Average Normal Low	15°	25°	32°
Record High	70°	79°	87°
Record Low	–26°	–10°	14°
Average Precipitation	1.8"	1.7"	1.5"

■ WESTERN SLOPE
based on Grand Junction

	March	April	May
Average Normal High	56°	66°	76°
Average Normal Low	31°	39°	48°
Record High	81°	89°	94°
Record Low	–5°	–11°	26°
Average Precipitation	0.9"	0.8"	0.9"

■ S. COLORADO
based on Alamosa

	March	April	May
Average Normal High	49°	59°	68°
Average Normal Low	16°	24°	33°
Record High	73°	80°	85°
Record Low	–20°	–6°	11°
Average Precipitation	0.4"	0.5"	0.7"

Source: National Weather Service.
Degrees are in Fahrenheit. Results based on data collected 1961–1990.

lingering cold to the north, and strong jet stream winds from the west.

The Jet Stream

What is the jet stream? It's best to imagine it as a long winding river of fast-moving air. This river of air is at its strongest at an altitude of five to six miles above the earth's surface. At that height the jet stream is above the friction-inducing effects of the ground, but below the stable air of the stratosphere, and can reach speeds of up to 200 miles per hour. The winds are not always that strong or fast, but rather become concentrated into narrow bands of very potent winds. Think of a river of water. The general flow of the river moves along at a fairly uniform speed, but there are certain narrow places, such as curves and rapids, where the water moves much faster. Those are like jet streams. If you paddle a canoe through that river, the tricky spots are those "jet stream" areas. In the atmosphere, the jet-stream winds are where conditions change very quickly. When a jet stream flows over Colorado, the result is usually a big change in the weather.

In Colorado, our 54 mountains over 14,000 feet (called "fourteeners") and their thirteen- and twelve-thousand-foot cousins can really create a maelstrom in the jet stream. Instead of a river like the South Platte on the eastern plains, think of one

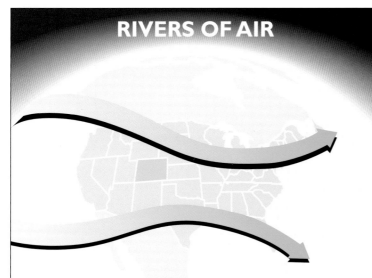

Jet stream winds circle the world like great rivers of air. Flowing from west to east, the strongest winds are concentrated into narrow bands where wind speeds may reach 200 miles per hour. Colorado's mountains create turbulence in the jet stream.

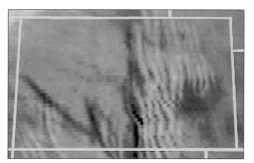

Jet stream turbulence is visible in this satellite image of Colorado.

of our Rocky Mountain streams. Just as the water bends and twists its way through falls and rapids on its way down the mountain, the jet-stream winds have to negotiate their way over and around our mountains. The entire volume of air from the surface well up into the stratosphere has to squeeze its way over Colorado. When strong jet-stream winds are whipping above Colorado, it's just like rafting down the Royal Gorge—get set for wild times!

Springtime Storms

So let's whip up a springtime storm system and watch how it happens. First, a moist, warm flow of air departs the Texas Gulf coast and begins to travel northward, carried by steady southerly breezes. On the weather map, you might notice a warm front or a band of thundershowers moving north toward Oklahoma. Meanwhile, a chilly pool of Canadian air is swirling down from northern Montana, with an eye toward spending a few days in Colorado. To the west, airline pilots at 30,000 feet over California are trying to dodge strong jet-stream winds in order to keep their passengers comfortable. We have all the ingredients for a major spring storm! During the next thirty-six hours, the strong winds over California cross Nevada, buffet skiers in the Wasatch Mountains of Utah, and howl high above western Colorado. Those winds by themselves would be enough to bring some moderate snows to our western mountains, but there is more excitement to come.

Warm moist air from the south and the chilly air from the north begin to close in on eastern Colorado. Temperatures fall over Wyoming, while folks in the Oklahoma Panhandle and southeastern Colorado open their windows to get a breath of fresh spring air into the house. Soon an extreme contrast in temperature exists from Wyoming to New Mexico, perhaps as much as forty to fifty degrees. This temperature contrast is not a stable condition due to the vastly different densities of the heavy cold air and lighter warm air. Trouble is brewing!

Don't be fooled by warm springtime days—wait until after Mother's Day to plant your garden.

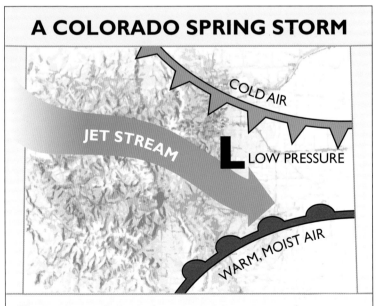

A COLORADO SPRING STORM

COLD AIR

JET STREAM

L LOW PRESSURE

WARM, MOIST AIR

The jet stream brings a low-pressure system to the eastern plains. The stage is now set for a spring storm. Cold air from the north is swirled together with warm, moist air from the Gulf of Mexico. The result can be snow, rain, hail, or tornadoes.

Cirrus clouds

Lenticular clouds

As the jet stream winds whip over the mountains, feathery cirrus clouds are the forerunners of the events about to unfold. These thin ice crystal clouds are blown and sculpted into eerie shapes called lenticular or "flying saucer" clouds along the Front Range. These lens- or saucer-shaped clouds are excellent signs of strong winds aloft and foretell a big change in the weather. The jet-stream winds have to squeeze their way over the mountains, but then the bottom drops out from under them on the plains. This causes the air pressure to drop and a low-pressure area forms just east of the Rockies (meteorologists call this a "lee-side" low).

We now have a developing low-pressure system, with warm, moist air to the south and cold air to the north. The ingredients are there: now mix together and bake! As the different air masses swirl inward toward the low, the air is forced to rise. This rising air cools, the moisture condenses into clouds, rain, and snow—and a storm is born! Depending on the intensity of the jet stream and the degree of contrast between the air masses, the storm may be a headliner or it may end up as a minor affair. The storm system will build over Colorado, but then drift off to the east to bring rain, snow, or thunderstorms to our neighbors on the plains.

March and April are the snowiest months of the year along the Front Range and offer some of the best skiing, thanks to a deep base of snow, fresh powder, and warmer temperatures—a great combination for skiers! It's ironic that many of the ski areas have to close down by mid-April due to lack of interest from out-of-state skiers—but for die-hard skiers, the result is great weather, great snow, and short lift-lines.

The World's Hail Capital

Eventually the warmth of springtime brings an end to the snow season and the beginning of the severe thunderstorm season, which brings a phenomenon familiar to most Coloradans—hail. The first hail and tornado weather usually arrives in early May. A major low-pressure system crossing the state in May can still bring heavy snow to the mountains, but the warm air drawn into southern Colorado ahead of the storm system usually produces severe thunderstorms on the eastern plains. In the early spring, the upper atmosphere is still very chilly, and a warm southerly surface wind will create unstable conditions in the air over Colorado. The warm, moist air easily rises up through the cold air aloft, much like a hot air balloon rises. As this air boils through the atmosphere, powerful thunderstorms develop. The cold air aloft allows for the formation of large hail. The eastern plains of Colorado are one of the hail capitals of the world, thanks in part to our elevation that puts us closer to the chilly air aloft, and in part to the mountains, which help to focus thunderstorm development.

It is not uncommon for storms to dump hail the size of golf balls or even softballs somewhere on the eastern plains each year. Throughout the state, hailstorms regularly damage crops, roofs, and even cars. The largest hailstone on record occurred in Coffeyville, Kansas, in 1970, and was the size of a head of lettuce!

HOW DO HAILSTONES FORM?

Ice crystals fall through cooled water droplets in a thunderstorm.

Water droplets freeze to the ice crystal, forming a "graupel."

As the graupel is held aloft by updrafts within the thunderstorm, more and more water droplets freeze to the graupel in layers and it becomes a hailstone.

The hailstone grows in size. When it becomes too heavy, or the updraft weakens, it falls to earth.

Most hailstones are less than half an inch in size, but some can become as large as a softball.

Twister Season

Another springtime visitor to Colorado is the tornado. The peak season for twisters in our state is from late May through June. Tornadoes are most likely to occur during this time due to the combination of strong temperature contrasts, which help create the thunderstorms and strong winds aloft that help to create a rotating monster called a "supercell." These thunderstorms feature a spinning motion that helps to inspire the smaller but vastly more intense rotation of the tornado. Supercell thunderstorms may form near the Denver area, but are more common farther to the east where the flat terrain allows the wind currents to really get organized into a large rotating system. The supercells that are born in Colorado roar off to the east and really cause headaches for our neighbors in Kansas, Oklahoma, and Nebraska. Although we can get large and damaging tornadoes in Colorado, they are less common here than in the states to our east. Our higher elevation tends to make our air a little drier, so even supercell thunderstorms in Colorado tend to be smaller than those in the central plains. Most Colorado tornadoes are small and short-lived, often lasting only five to ten minutes. The vast majority of our tornadoes have winds of 100 miles per hour or less. A few, such as the one that hit Limon in 1990, can reach wind speeds of over 200 miles per hour.

Fortunately the biggest tornadoes in Colorado tend to occur where the population is smallest—out on the far eastern plains. That may be small comfort if you live in Haxtun, Holyoke, or Holly, but take heart—no one has been killed by a tornado in the state of Colorado since the 1960s! Just the same, with our rapidly increasing

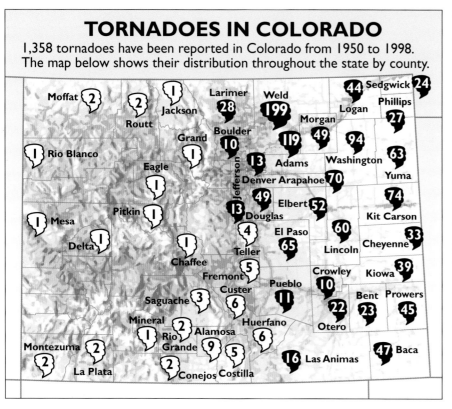

TORNADOES IN COLORADO

1,358 tornadoes have been reported in Colorado from 1950 to 1998. The map below shows their distribution throughout the state by county.

Moffat 2
Jackson 2
Larimer 28
Weld 199
Sedgwick 44
Sedgwick 24
Phillips 27
Routt
Logan
Morgan
Grand 1
Boulder 10
Adams 119
Morgan 49
Washington 94
Rio Blanco 1
Eagle 1
Jefferson 13
Denver
Arapahoe 70
Yuma 63
Pitkin 1
Jefferson 13
Elbert 49
Elbert 52
Kit Carson 74
Mesa 1
Douglas 13
Delta 1
Douglas 4
El Paso 65
Lincoln 60
Cheyenne 33
Chaffee 1
Teller
Fremont 5
Crowley 10
Kiowa 39
Saguache 3
Custer 6
Pueblo 11
Bent 22
Prowers 45
Mineral 2
Alamosa
Huerfano 6
Otero 23
Montezuma 2
Rio Grande 9
Costilla 5
Las Animas 16
Baca 47
La Plata 2
Conejos 2
Costilla

Tornado Safety

Some rules of tornado safety, such as opening windows, have been abandoned. In the past it was thought that opening the windows would help to equalize the pressure difference created by the near-vacuum of the tornado. By equalizing the pressure, the house would not explode outward as the tornado passed by. Research has shown that most houses are leaky enough that the air escapes anyway, and that nearly all of the damage from a tornado is caused by the tremendous winds, not the pressure difference. Opening the windows does little to protect your property, and may put you in harm's way as you waste valuable time trying to close windows rather than immediately seeking shelter. The most likely result of opening the windows will just be a living room full of rain!

Another old bit of advice about tornadoes was to hide in the southwest corner of the basement. The logic here was that most tornadoes come from the southwest and move toward the northeast. When you hid in the southwest corner of the basement, you would be safe because the house would be lifted up and dropped toward the northeast and you would be left unharmed and looking up at open sky.

It sounds good in theory, but in practice this scenario seldom occurs. Besides, some tornadoes come from the west or northwest —and how would one know for sure? Perhaps the more important point is that not everyone has the same home construction design. If your house is a split-level with a walkout basement on the southwest side, then that certainly would not be the best place to seek shelter. The best advice is to survey your home carefully and try to locate the sturdiest part of your house. It might be under the stairs, or under a workbench in the middle of the basement, or perhaps in an interior bathroom (the pipes add extra strength to the walls). Find the strongest part of your home and go there when a tornado threatens. The best thing to do is to practice a family tornado drill in the same way you would make a fire safety plan—especially if you have small children.

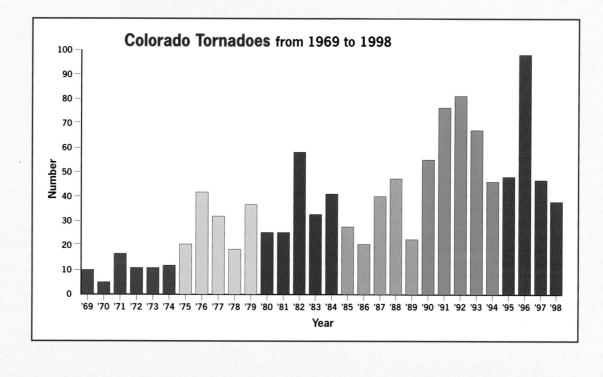

Tornado near Watkins

population, it's important to know what to do and where to go in the event of a tornado.

There are many rules about tornado safety that have been around since I was a kid. Some of the rules are still accurate and worthwhile to follow; others are not. The best way to ensure your safety during a tornado is to simply "get low and protect your head." This is easy for even a young child to remember, and it could save your life. Getting as low as possible, no matter where you are, decreases the chance that you will be hit by flying debris—the greatest hazard from a tornado. Covering your head and eyes will also help protect you from anything that might be whipping around in the strong winds. If you're in a building, go into the basement or the lowest floor. Protect your head by getting under something sturdy like a bench or heavy table. If you're outside or in open country, get into a ditch.

Springtime in the Rockies

Not all of springtime is cold and snowy or warm and violent. Much of it is very enjoyable as the promise of warm temperatures and more sunshine is at hand. Coloradans enjoy the first signs of spring after months of a landscape that is either covered with snow or dry and brown. Although warm spring days may seem benign, they too can be a source of worry. By the end of winter, vast amounts of snow have piled onto the mountainsides. A rapid warm-up quickly brings that moisture

back down. During late April through early June, a major concern in many mountain towns is flooding from snowmelt. The worst scenario is when a very snowy winter and early spring are suddenly replaced by a week of sunshine and highs in the eighties. The snowpack can diminish at a rate of several inches per day, and all that icy cold water fills mountain streams and reservoirs quickly. If we have a series of warm days followed by a soggy spring

14

storm, snowmelt flooding can create a serious threat. Many of our great whitewater rafting rivers are very cold, high, and dangerous in May and early June. Newcomers to this exciting sport should wait until July to hit the rivers—and even seasoned rafters and kayakers take special care in the spring.

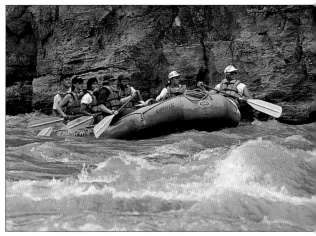

Gardeners, too, can often be fooled by the warm springtime days. The best advice I can give to Colorado gardeners is: Don't plant your garden before Mother's Day! It may be very enticing on those warm weekends of late April when those seed catalogs arrive in your mailbox, but don't be fooled! The average last date of freezing temperatures in the Denver area is May 5. Snow is still possible in Denver until about the

middle of May or even early June. Many a beautiful late-April garden has had to be replanted in mid-May thanks to a nasty cold snap! And if you live above six-thousand feet in elevation, you may want to wait even longer, until closer to June. The foothills often have to endure a couple of soggy snowstorms at least through the second week of May. But don't worry—there will be plenty of warm days to come as summer arrives in Colorado.

Colorado SUMMER

The summer season is a busy time for weather forecasters —a fact that I learned quickly when I first came to Colorado. What a wild ride I had! In 1991 my wife, Cindy, and I were on our way to Denver, where I was to start my new job at 9NEWS. We stopped for gas in Burlington, Colorado, where the temperatures were in the high eighties with a brisk southerly wind, fairly high humidity, and a beautiful sunny sky. As we drove on toward Denver, a few puffy cumulus clouds began to grow and darken. Somewhere between Limon and Bennett, those clouds gathered together into a dark gray mass. Lightning flickered in the distance and static crackled as we tuned in to KOA radio for a weather update, and we learned that Denver and its vicinity were being hit by a severe thunderstorm that brought heavy rain, hail, and even some funnel cloud sightings.

By the time we arrived in Denver, however, the storm had rumbled on to the east, leaving behind a late-afternoon rainbow in the eastern sky behind the city skyline. We thought at the time that we had experienced a rare "once-in-a-while" storm, but soon discovered that this type of weather was pretty much a daily occurrence along the Front Range! During my first summer in Colorado, I recall only one or two days from mid-June through July that we did not have severe thunderstorms, hail, or tornado sightings. I manned the weather operation at 9NEWS with veteran weatherman Bill Kuster, and we

DAYS OF SUMMER

FRONT RANGE
based on Denver

	June	July	August
Average Normal High	81°	88°	86°
Average Normal Low	52°	59°	57°
Record High	104°	103°	105°
Record Low	30°	42°	40°
Average Precipitation	2.1"	2.0"	1.7"

HIGH COUNTRY
based on Aspen*

	June	July	August
Average Normal High	74°	80°	78°
Average Normal Low	38°	44°	43°
Record High	93°	94°	92°
Record Low	15°	31°	27°
Average Precipitation	1.2"	1.4"	1.7"

WESTERN SLOPE
based on Grand Junction

	June	July	August
Average Normal High	87°	93°	90°
Average Normal Low	57°	64°	62°
Record High	105°	105°	103°
Record Low	34°	44°	43°
Average Precipitation	0.5"	0.6"	0.9"

S. COLORADO
based on Alamosa

	June	July	August
Average Normal High	78°	82°	79°
Average Normal Low	41°	48°	45°
Record High	95°	96°	90°
Record Low	24°	30°	29°
Average Precipitation	0.6"	1.1"	1.2"

Source: National Weather Service.
Degrees are in Fahrenheit. Results based on data collected 1961–1990.
*Source: International Station Meteorological Climate Summary, Version 4.0.

almost never got a dinner break! That summer was a particularly rough one, but most years feature an almost daily dose of heavy thunderstorms somewhere over the eastern plains of Colorado.

Convection

The reason for this abundance of thundery weather can be traced to our mountains. You could almost think of those twelve- to thirteen-thousand-foot peaks as giant heating elements. To a great extent, the sun's energy does not warm the atmosphere directly. Instead, the solar energy (meteorologists call it "short-wave" radiation) that reaches the top of the atmosphere goes through a series of events before actually heating the air. Some of the energy is reflected back into space directly by clouds and dust in the air. Another portion of the energy is absorbed by oceans and heats the water. Some energy is used to evaporate water and is stored as latent heat (to be released later when the water vapor condenses back into liquid). Finally, some of the energy heats rocks as well as sand, grass, fields, and forests. The heat from the ocean surface and the land masses is the primary source of heat for the atmosphere. This warmth radiates from the land and sea and heats the air just above it, similar to the way in which a stove top heats a pan. The warmer air becomes less dense (due to the molecules being more energized and moving farther apart) and the air will rise—just like a hot air balloon. This rising air is called "convection" and is the key to most of our summertime stormy weather.

Convection from typical daytime heating causes the majority of our thunderstorms in Colorado. By midafternoon, the sun has heated the ground for hours and temperatures near the surface have reached a peak. The warm ground heats the air to a significant extent, and rising columns of air called "thermals" bubble up all over the place. Thermals are what glider pilots and soaring birds love to find, as they provide lift. As the air rises, there is less pressure above the earth's surface and the bubble of air expands further. This expansion causes the air bubble (or "parcel of air," as meteorologists call it) to cool at a rate of about 5.5 degrees per thousand feet of ascent. Cooler air cannot hold as much water vapor as warm air, so

Even on the hottest summer day, a tremendous blizzard can be swirling around just three or four miles above your head.

moisture begins to condense in the form of clouds. Often the condensation occurs rather abruptly at a certain altitude and temperature, which is why the puffy clouds of a summer sky may develop a flat bottom. The flat bottom marks the exact height where moisture in the air parcel begins to condense from water vapor back into liquid water—a height that meteorologists call the "lifted condensation level" (LCL).

The role the mountains play in all of this is to provide an elevated platform for the initial heating of the air. Rather than an air parcel being heated at sea level and having to bubble all the way, up to thousands of feet, to reach the LCL, the mountains put that heating element much higher into the atmosphere. Clouds form very quickly over the mountains during a summer morning, and then those clouds can drift off over the plains by midafternoon. The mountains serve as a "thunderstorm factory" because once condensation occurs, a chain reaction begins to occur. Nature has a "give-and-take" process that is called "latent heating," a process that I referred to earlier. Simply put, it takes

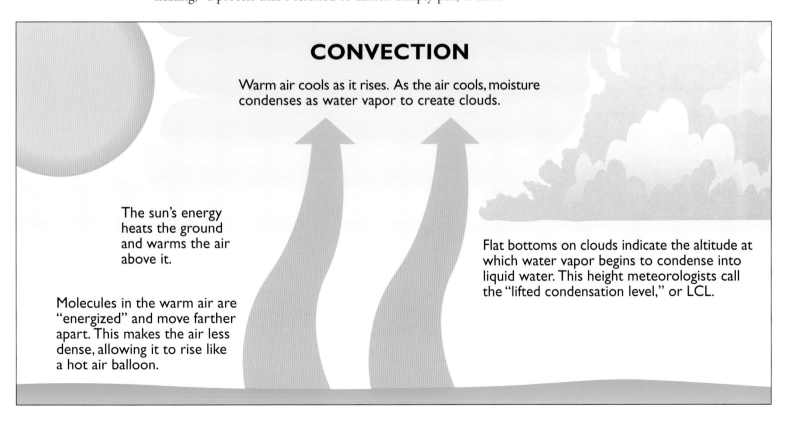

CONVECTION

Warm air cools as it rises. As the air cools, moisture condenses as water vapor to create clouds.

The sun's energy heats the ground and warms the air above it.

Molecules in the warm air are "energized" and move farther apart. This makes the air less dense, allowing it to rise like a hot air balloon.

Flat bottoms on clouds indicate the altitude at which water vapor begins to condense into liquid water. This height meteorologists call the "lifted condensation level," or LCL.

energy to evaporate water, but that energy is returned when the water condenses back into liquid. When you step out of the shower, think of the chill you feel before you towel off. That chill is the heat your body is giving up to evaporate the water from your skin. When water changes state from liquid to gas, it requires energy. When it changes back from gas to liquid, that energy is released. So, in the atmosphere, water vapor condensing into a cloud actually gives off heat. That warming makes the bubble or parcel of air buoyant once again and it will continue to rise higher into the sky. As it rises, there is less pressure, more expansion, the parcel cools, and additional water vapor condenses to form more clouds. This of course means that more latent heat is released, warming the parcel again. It rises further, creating more clouds, and continues the process high into the sky—an atmospheric chain reaction.

Convection is the key to most of our summertime stormy weather.

As the clouds grow, some of the water condenses into droplets of water, but much of it skips that phase and forms tiny ice crystals. By the time you reach an altitude of sixteen to eighteen thousand feet, temperatures generally stay below freezing, even in the middle of summer. The tiny droplets of water and crystals of ice swirl around inside the cloud like a gigantic atmospheric

traffic jam. As in a traffic jam, collisions occur and the droplets and ice crystals lock together like car bumpers. As more and more tiny bits of water crash into each other, raindrops and snowflakes form and grow. It may offer you some cool comfort to know that even on the hottest summer day, a tremendous blizzard can be swirling around just three or four miles above your head!

Eventually, the raindrops and snowflakes become large enough that they can no longer float and they fall to earth. It is seldom a direct flight, however, as upward-moving wind currents created by the convection and latent heat release, called "updrafts," may keep the rain and snow suspended in the clouds much like you would blow a feather up into the air and keep it there with each breath. But like a feather, the drops and flakes tend to go up and down and swirl around until they finally drop to earth. This up-and-down motion has all sorts of ramifications as it helps to create lightning, hail, and strong winds.

Lightning, Thunder, and Hail

Lightning is caused by vigorous motion inside the cloud. As the tiny drops of rain and crystals of snow swirl around, electrons are torn away from their surfaces, and huge amounts of static electricity form. A good analogy is to think about when you shuffle your feet across a carpet. The warmth that you feel on the bottom of your feet is caused by friction. The friction creates static electricity that you see as a spark that jumps when you touch the light switch or another person. Zapping one of my older sisters was one of my favorite things to do when I was a kid—little did I know that it would lead to a career in weather!

In the thunderstorm cloud, the static charge grows until it is so strong that it overcomes any resistance in the air and a giant spark of lightning is created. But does the lightning move down from the cloud, or up from the ground? The answer is BOTH! If you look at a battery, you know that electricity has both positive and negative charges. These opposites are attracted to each other. As the turbulence in a thunderstorm strips off the negatively charged electrons, they tend to collect at the base of the thunderstorm, giving it a net negative charge. This negative charge attracts, or induces, a positive charge on the ground beneath the thunderstorm. This positive charge will follow the thunderstorm like an "electric shadow." Eventually the amount of negative and positive charge will grow to be so great that they begin to move closer together. The negatively charged electrons move fairly easily down from the cloud base in a thin, virtually invisible zigzagging path called a "stepped leader." The positive charges need a little help to move and they travel best over some type of conductor, such as a tall metal tower, a tree, a golf club—or a person! When the positive charge and the negative charge finally meet, that is when the brilliant flash of light (called the return stroke) actually occurs. So the next time someone asks if lightning travels up or down, let them know that it does both! Even

(Continued on page 24)

The Tornado Dance

A great big blob of hot air floats over Denver. "Oh, man, this is great! I really love making everybody hot and sweaty! I don't think I'll ever leave."

But cool air up in Canada has a different idea. "You know, I am way too cool to be stuck up here in Canada. I think I'll cruise on down to Denver and cool everybody off!"

Kids Love Weather!

What could be more fun to a gym full of kids than learning how to do the Tornado Dance? And getting a fascinating lesson in weather balloons, radiosondes, and Colorado storm formations along the way?

Each week, meteorologist Mike Nelson travels to Denver-area elementary schools to talk to kids and share his stories and expertise. With a trunkful of weather-related materials for youngsters to examine, he talks about his job as a forecaster and provides fun but important facts about Colorado weather.

Weather forecasters depend upon information they receive daily from weather balloons launched from about 500 locations around the globe. Each day these balloons are released at exactly the same time—at noon and midnight Greenwich Mean Time, which is 5 a.m. and 5 p.m. Mountain Standard Time. Each balloon carries a little box called a radiosonde, which measures air pressure, temperature, and humidity.

The balloons are also closely tracked to determine wind speed and direction.

The balloons rise more than 15 miles above the earth, and data is radioed back to earth. Eventually each balloon bursts and falls back to earth with the radiosonde still attached. There's a small chance, Mike will tell his listeners, that a deflated weather balloon and radiosonde could indeed fall into your backyard. When that happens, instructions on the box tell the finder how to package it up and mail it back. "You could be the

"Get lost!" the hot air says to the cool air. "Go on back to Canada!"

"No way!" answers the cool air. "I'm way too cool to be pushed around by you!"

A big fight occurs between the cool air and the hot air, forcing air up above them to rise. This rising air billows into great big thunderstorm clouds. The air inside the developing thunderstorm rises like smoke through a chimney. A jet stream above the thunderstorm makes it begin to spin.

smartest kid on the block!" Mike says. "No one else will know what it is, and you'll be able to tell the other kids all about it!"

To the delight of his audience, Mike also demonstrates how a summer storm— even a tornado—can build quickly on a warm Colorado day. "When I was a kid growing up in Wisconsin, I always wanted to stand right next to the window and watch the storm come in," he exclaims. "My mother would pull me by the collar down to the basement, but when she wasn't looking, I'd scurry up the stairs to get another look!" During a tornado watch, however, it's very important to be in a safe place away from windows or open spaces, so Mike would ultimately have to follow his parents' orders. Nevertheless, his love of stormy weather was born.

Often Mike will ask a student to come up to the front of the room to help demonstrate how a particular piece of equipment works.

Kids learn that there are some easy things they can do to set up a small weather station in their own backyard.

The most popular part of Mike's demonstration is the infamous Tornado Dance. With the help of a "cool" pair of sunglasses and a bit of a swagger, Mike shows kids how hot, blustery air from the south and cool, forceful air from the north can meet over Colorado to create powerful storms. He then illustrates how the whirling force of a tornado builds and spins—and even the audience gets a little dizzy!

One of the most enjoyable aspects of Mike's job as a meteorologist is the chance to get out and talk to kids every week. Often the children will catch a glimpse of themselves and their friends and teachers on the evening news. With Mike Nelson, kids learn all kinds of interesting facts about Colorado weather—and a few unexpected things as well!

The spinning gets faster and smaller and faster and smaller, just like a figure skater pulling his or her arms in, and a tornado begins to form. The funnel forms way up in the middle of the thunderstorm and then travels on down until it reaches the ground. And that, boys and girls, is how to do the Tornado Dance!

more astonishing is that all of the action I've just described takes place in a tiny fraction of a second.

The big danger, of course, is being in or near the conductor or vehicle that allows the charges to connect and flow. That's why you should never stand outside in an open area during a thunderstorm. Those positive charges will travel up to the top of your head and flag down any wayward negative charges looking for a thrill. Unfortunately, that thrill can kill—in an average year, more people are killed by lightning than by tornadoes or hurricanes. The best advice is to get indoors, even if the storm clouds seem distant. Lightning can easily travel several miles and can strike even if the sky above is clear—the so-called "bolt from the blue"!

Lightning may travel up and down the zigzag path of the stepped leader several times, back and forth like water sloshing in a tub. The flashes are so very quick that our eyes cannot discern the individual flashes and instead we see a flicker of lightning over and over. Studies have shown that lightning does indeed strike twice; in fact, one flicker may actually be as many as a dozen multiple flashes in the same lightning channel, all in the course of a split second.

Lightning is also extraordinarily hot—about fifty thousand

degrees Fahrenheit or five times the temperature of the surface of the sun. As this bolt of energy races through the air, it rapidly heats the air for a fraction of a second. This heating causes the surrounding air to rapidly expand and then contract as the heat source disappears. The contraction slaps the molecules of air back together, creating a shock wave that we hear as thunder. Thunder can be scary, but is not dangerous or damaging itself (although your family dog might disagree—dogs are often petrified of thunder!). In fact, thunder can be useful. The sound waves take about five seconds to travel one mile, while the lightning is seen instantaneously. So when you see the lightning, begin to count slowly until you hear the thunder. When you hear the thunder, divide the number of seconds counted by five to get the approximate distance from you to the lightning. For example, let's say you see a flash of lightning and can count to fifteen before you hear the thunder. Fifteen divided by five is three,

LIGHTNING

Vigorous movement within the storm cloud creates large amounts of static electricity. Positive and negative charges gather throughout the cloud.

Opposite charges are "induced" on the ground. The opposite charges in the cloud and on the ground move toward each other.

A lightning flash occurs when the opposite charges meet.

The bolt of energy rapidly heats the air for a fraction of a second. This causes the surrounding air to expand and contract, creating a shock wave we hear as thunder.

Lightning produces an intense radio signal called a "sferic." Special antennae detect the signal and relay it to a computer, which quickly plots it on a map.

so the lightning strike is three miles away. This is a useful tool, because if the amount of time between the flash and the thunder is growing smaller, it may be a good idea to stop what you're doing and get inside where it's safe.

If you watch 9NEWS in the summertime, you may see our lightning strike display system. Each cloud-to-ground lightning strike is shown as a small cross sign on the map. This system works on a fascinating principle. Lightning strikes create a brief but very intense radio signal called "sferic." This signal is the static sound that you hear when listening to an AM radio station during a thunderstorm. This signal, or sferic, has a unique signature for a cloud-to-ground lightning strike. Special antennae have been set up all over the United States to detect this special radio signal. When a lightning strike occurs, the sferic is picked up by many of these antennae at virtually the same time (the signal travels at the speed of light). By triangulating between each of these antennae, we can quickly pinpoint the location of the lightning. The calculations are all done by one computer, and the system is so fast that you will likely see the lightning out your window, see the strike displayed on 9NEWS, and then hear the thunder! It is not unusual for Colorado to get ten to fifteen thousand lightning strikes from one single stormy day. This system is used here not only for television, but is also

very important in the detection of forest fires caused by lightning. Forest rangers can refer to the lightning strike map and immediately send aircraft out to look for signs of smoke in areas where lightning has been intense. This system is also used by NASA and is considered a "launch critical" device—in other words, if lightning is detected near the Kennedy Space Center, the launch will be delayed. The lightning detecting systems are used all over the nation now, but 9NEWS was the very first television station in the country to have such a system.

Hail occurs not only in the springtime but well into the summer as well. In the last chapter, we showed how hail is formed as a result of a swirling combination of snowflakes, raindrops, or "supercooled water" inside a thunderstorm (under certain conditions, water may stay in liquid form even at temperatures well below freezing). As the wild wind motions throw tiny ice crystals or even particles of dust around, they bump into the supercooled water and form tiny little nuggets of ice. As these nuggets are tossed about, they bump into other ice crystals and

more supercooled water, combine, and gradually turn into hailstones. The thunderstorm updraft supports the upward motion of the hail, while the downward motion is of course caused by gravity. The hail goes up and down and all around the inside of the thunderstorm — I like to think of the flight of the hailstone as a giant juggling act in the sky! Scientists estimate that it takes an updraft of at least 100 miles per hour to keep aloft a baseball-sized hailstone.

Downbursts and Microbursts

Another dangerous weather phenomenon in the thunderstorm arsenal is the downburst or microburst. These strong straight-line winds differ from a tornado in formation, but the result can be just as damaging. Downburst winds are caused by the downward rush of rain-cooled air from the base of the thunderstorm. As the rain and hail fall from the storm, evaporation and cooling occur. This cooling makes the air heavier and it sinks rapidly toward the ground. When the air hits the ground, it fans out in all directions, swirling away from the thunderstorm base like a pencil rolling off a desk. This swirling air has a horizontal axis of rotation, as opposed to the vertical one of a tornado. Nevertheless, the winds of a downburst can reach speeds of hurricane strength (75 miles per hour) and may even exceed 100 miles per hour. These winds can do great damage and even cause death.

Recent studies show that strong downburst wind events may actually get some of their momentum from the jet stream. Satellite photos

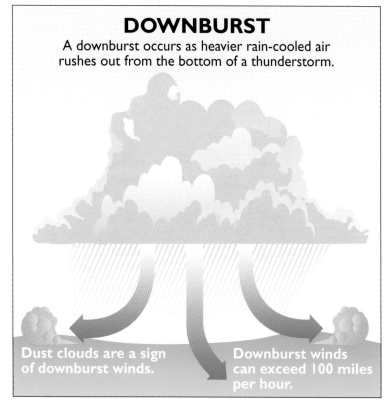

DOWNBURST

A downburst occurs as heavier rain-cooled air rushes out from the bottom of a thunderstorm.

Dust clouds are a sign of downburst winds.

Downburst winds can exceed 100 miles per hour.

indicate that just before a powerful downburst, the top of the thunderstorm cloud may actually sink several thousand feet. It is almost as if the storm is taking a deep breath and exhaling out this big blast of wind. Research shows that a portion of the jet-stream winds may actually travel down through the thunderstorm and race out from the bottom of the storm. This "shove from above" gives the thunderstorm winds an extra boost of power. Large-scale damaging downburst events are called "derechos"—a Spanish word meaning "straight ahead"—and are often associated with this impulse of jet stream-winds that traverse through the thunderstorm.

Another type of downburst that we hear a lot about is the microburst. This straight-line wind is on a smaller scale than a downburst, but is essentially the same phenomenon. Microbursts are very common in Colorado, due in part to the small, scattered, but intense thunderstorms that we have. There are two types of microbursts: dry ones and wet ones. Obviously the wet ones are associated with heavy rainfall and the dry ones are not. We often have dry microbursts in Colorado because our atmosphere tends to have low humidity. Rain that falls from a cloud may evaporate well before reaching the ground. Such rain is called "virga" and is a common sight in our summertime sky. Virga is the tattered cloud edge or ragged look that you see at the bottom of a thunderstorm. When the rain evaporates, it cools the surrounding air, making the air more dense and causing the air to drop quickly to the ground. The air then hits the surface and fans out in all directions. On television we sometimes refer to microbursts as "outflow boundaries." These strong, gusty winds—sometimes reaching fifty to seventy-five miles an hour—can blow lawn furniture, patio umbrellas, and other light- to medium-weight objects all over, but yet bring nary a drop of rain. Wet

Virga

microbursts, on the other hand, have enough moisture to produce strong winds and heavy rainfall, and are sometimes mistaken for tornadoes because the rain obscures visibility so completely that no one can tell if there was a funnel or not.

Microbursts are major hazards to aviation and have caused several airline accidents. Pilots always try to take off and land into the wind—by flying into the wind, a greater amount of air flows over the wing surfaces to create lift. This is very important, especially during landing when speed and engine power are reduced. If a microburst occurs near an airport, it can suddenly cause the wind to shift in the opposite direction. A plane landing into the wind will quickly have a tailwind instead. The plane can lose lift and begin to fall too fast, ending up short of the runway. If there is time, the pilot can increase engine power to gain more lift, but it takes jet engines a few seconds to wind up. Those few seconds are not available when the plane is already close to the ground. Major airports, including Denver International Airport (DIA), have

Microburst

Flying in Colorado: Exhilaration and Calculated Risk

"Any month has its risks for flying in Colorado," says Nick Carter, meteorologist and veteran pilot. "During the spring and summer months, turbulence is a problem (and always seems to occur just prior to lunchtime!). On summer afternoons, it's particularly important to watch out for thunderstorms."

Cold weather presents its own set of challenges. "The air tends to be much smoother in the winter," Carter notes, "but ice can be a problem. You can also encounter significant turbulence over the mountains. The jet stream blows from west to east at approximately 55 to 60 miles per hour, and the air tumbles over the mountains like a stream tumbles over rocks."

All pilots are required to obtain weather information before they leave the airport. Many of the larger planes have their own Doppler radar, on-board lightning detectors, and equipment that heats the plane's wings to melt the ice. Some airlines even have their own weather forecasters, though any pilot can talk to the air traffic tower for updates.

Carter has been a meteorologist at 9KUSA for 14 years. Originally from Chicago, he recalls that his first love was flying. "When I was a kid," he says, "I used to love to watch the planes fly in and out of O'Hare Airport." He received his bachelor's degree in meteorology from Northern Illinois University and advises future meteorologists to take classes in journalism and speech. Carter also volunteers with the Colorado chapter of the Ninety-Nines, an organization founded by women pilots to help inform and calm people who are afraid of flying.

Aside from weather risks, Carter finds flying in Colorado exhilarating. On one flight from Wyoming, he recalls, "the air looked like a giant pond, and the clouds looked like lily pads. I felt like a big fish flying through it."

Nick Carter

sophisticated wind-measuring equipment that can identify developing microburst conditions and warn pilots ahead of time. With that warning, a pilot might elect to circle for a while until the microburst is over, or even go to a different airport.

Flash Floods

As the summer rolls on, the main threat from thunderstorms switches from hail, microbursts, and tornadoes to heavy rain and flash flooding. By mid-July, the jet-stream winds become quite sluggish over the United States, as the strongest winds aloft tend to be found over Canada. The lack of strong winds at twenty-five to thirty thousand feet means that thunderstorms do not have much in the way of steering currents. Storms that develop tend to move at only five to fifteen miles per hour and therefore can dump a tremendous amount of rain over a particular area. It is not uncommon during mid to late summer to have three to six inches of rain dumped in just a few hours. This kind of downpour cannot all soak into the soil, so it runs off into ditches, dry washes, and low-lying areas. Flash flooding is the number-one weather hazard in Colorado from mid-July through early September.

The combination of light winds aloft and our mountainous terrain creates some intense downpours, with tragic consequences. The Big Thompson Flood in 1976 remains one of the worst weather disasters in Colorado's and even the nation's history. The weather situation on that day was a combination tailor-made to produce incredible localized rainfall amounts. Very light winds aloft teamed

The Big Thompson Flood

with a moist easterly wind at the surface to create a thunderstorm machine that stalled for hours between Estes Park and Loveland. The easterly winds served as a moisture conveyor that fed humid air into the base of the storm. The mountains forced that air to rise, but the light winds aloft could not blow the storm away from the mountains. The result was over a foot of rain falling over Glen Haven and Glen Comfort. Massive amounts of water swept down through the Big Thompson Canyon, sweeping unwary campers and homeowners to their deaths.

Flash Flood Safety Tips

A few safety tips are worth mentioning in the event of flash floods. First, know your area and understand the risk, if any, of flash flooding. If you live in or are camping in an area that is prone to flooding, have an emergency plan in place and discuss it with your family—even the youngest members. Be on the lookout during the mid to late summer months for signs of thunderstorms. If the storms are slow to move away, there may be a potential for flash flooding. Remember that in mountainous areas, it doesn't need to be raining right where you are, but rather upstream from you, to cause a flash flood. If you have access to television or radio, stay up-to-date with the latest weather information. In the event of a flash flood, move very quickly to higher ground. If you are in your car, don't attempt to drive through a flooded area of unknown depth. Tragic accidents have occurred when people have tried to drive through a flooded area and then were swept away by the raging water. At the very least, your car may be completely flooded and totaled by water damage.

1997 Fort Collins flood

In the summer of 1997, a similar event on a slightly smaller scale hit on the southwest side of Fort Collins. This intense, nearly stationary storm developed under conditions much the same as those twenty-one years earlier and created a wall of water that broke through a railroad bed and blasted into a mobile home park. It was an eerie scene as rescuers fought raging water and dodged the flames from ruptured propane tanks in order to save the residents from the rising water. Despite their courageous efforts, seven people lost their lives.

Fire

Sometimes Colorado's late summer weather problem is fire, not rain. In dry years, a major weather concern is grass and forest fires. If weather conditions are moist in the spring, the growth of grass and underbrush is high. As the weather dries out, so does all the lush growth and it becomes excellent tinder for fires. Dry years can still feature thunderstorms, but they produce lots of lightning and very little rain. Lightning is a major cause of fires not just in Colorado, but over most of the Rockies. In recent years, forestry officials have adopted new policies about letting some of the natural fires burn if they pose little threat to people or property. The idea is to allow small fires to burn away some of the fuels on the forest

floor to minimize the chance of a catastrophic fire at a later time. This idea marked a big switch from the old "Smokey the Bear" policy of putting out all fires. It is a wise policy, but still offers the risk of a fire getting out of hand. Unfortunately, the explosive growth along the Front Range has put many homes into forested areas, which makes it impossible to let a fire burn in many locales. The Buffalo Creek fire of 1996, although it was man-made, was a scary example of what may happen in the future. That fire, spread by a hot, dry wind and fed on plentiful dry tinder, blew up into a raging conflagration. The heat from the flames was unusually intense and burned hot enough to sterilize the

> ### Fire Safety Tips
> During fire weather, stay tuned to the television and radio for updates and information about existing fires. If you live in an area that has a threat of fire, have a plan of action ready for your family and evacuate quickly when necessary. Consider getting a fireproof box or safe to hold important family documents and keepsakes. Clear away trees and brush from close proximity to your house, and make sure that your access road is in good shape for potential fire crews. Above all, please be extremely cautious with outdoor burning. A campfire caused the Buffalo Creek fire; it was left unattended because it was thought to be extinguished. We can't prevent lightning-caused forest fires, but Smokey the Bear is right about the human-caused kind: "Only you can prevent forest fires!"

soil. Seeds that normally are activated by a medium-sized fire were rendered lifeless. Heavy rains followed the fire a few weeks later, causing severe erosion. The area will struggle for decades to get plants to regenerate. That fire occurred in one of the few relatively unpopulated areas along the Front Range. Had it been just a few miles farther to the north, Evergreen and Conifer could have had a real tragedy.

Although dry weather makes forest fires a threat, it is the low humidity that makes summertime in Colorado so appealing. Unlike our neighbors to the east, we actually can go outdoors in relative comfort even on a really hot summer day. Our dry climate is a result of both altitude and location, location, location. Because we are about as far away from the ocean as one can get in the United States, moist air has a long way to travel to get here. Our high elevation blocks many of the moisture-laden storms from getting here, or weakens them and dries them out before they do. The result? Wonderful summertime comfort!

River Excitement: Rafting in Colorado

Anyone who's been on a rafting trip down a Colorado river will tell you—prepare for any weather imaginable. According to Dave Burch of Echo Canyon River Expeditions, river rafters may encounter thunderstorms, hail, heavy rain, or even snow during a summer run. Adding an adrenaline rush to an already exciting trip, Colorado's unpredictable weather has a plus side: "We run rain or shine, because you get wet anyway and it's still a great time!" exclaims Burch.

River-rafting season in Colorado runs from mid-April to the end of September. "July is the best month," says Burch. "You get a better combination of good weather and good water. In July, the Arkansas River is running from 1,000 to 2,000 cubic feet per second and the air temperature is 80 to 90 degrees."

Burch, who started rafting while an outdoor recreation major at Arizona State University, has been guiding rafting trips with his wife, Kim, down the Arkansas for over 20 years.

Although many rivers in Colorado are rafted every year, the Arkansas River is one of the most popular. The rapids along this route are classified from I to IV, with Class I water considered the calmest and Class IV water technical and demanding. Familiarity with water conditions is the key to safe rafting.

If you plan to take a river-rafting trip in Colorado, be sure that the river outfitter ensures your safety by providing professional guides and well-maintained equipment. Shorts and swimsuits are the best things to wear, although you may rent a wetsuit or wear raingear. Bring a change of warm clothes for after the trip.

Although the high waters in June offer a more exciting ride, the Arkansas mellows in early season and late summer, when Burch's company runs most of its float fishing trips. "We had one guest last year who caught 50 trout in three hours," Burch recalls. "It was catch and release, and he had a great time."

Our Friendly Dew Point

Our measure of the amount of moisture in the air is called the "dew point." The dew point is the temperature at which the air would be saturated with moisture and the relative humidity would be one-hundred percent. If the air temperature was eighty degrees and the dew point was sixty degrees, the air would have to cool to sixty in order for it to become saturated. Once the air is saturated, clouds, rain, snow, fog, or dew may occur. The latter is the reason it is called the dew point, as on a clear night the air cools down and dew gathers on the grass.

In Colorado, our dew points in the summer are usually in the thirties and forties. That is why we do not usually have morning dew like our neighbors in the Midwest and East. Sometimes dew points drop way down to the teens or single digits. This occurs when we have a strong southwest wind that comes from the desert. The air is already quite dry, but it dries out even further as it rides up and over the mountains. When the air is that dry, it is almost too dry and can make your eyes, skin, and nose dry out to the point of being very uncomfortable.

Most of the time, our low dew points are friendly and make it very pleasant to be outdoors. In contrast to Colorado having dew points in the forties, the Midwest and East usually sweat through dew points in the sixties and seventies all summer long. The old saying, "It's not the heat, but the humidity!" seldom applies in Colorado. In fact, dew points above sixty-five are rarely reported except way out on the eastern plains. When we get dew points in the fifties in Denver, we usually have heavy rains from thunderstorms.

Although our heat tends to be a "dry heat," the same can be said about an oven! We still get our share of sweltering days in Colorado. The all-time hottest day in Denver was August 8, 1878, when the thermometer soared to 105 degrees. The record high for the entire state is 118 degrees, recorded at Bennett on July 11, 1888. (There is some controversy about the accuracy of that reading, as some say the thermometer was not set up properly.) The next warmest reading for the state that day was only 105 degrees. So, depending upon which reference you check, you might also find the state record high listed at 114 degrees, set on July 11, 1954, at the town of Sedgwick. Frankly, when it's that hot, what's a few degrees among friends? But the good news about hot summer days is that by Labor Day, things begin to ease into autumn.

Colorado AUTUMN

Autumn is an enigma in Colorado. One of the most pleasant and certainly most beautiful times of year, it's also a time when the weather can't seem to make up its mind. Summer is over and winter hasn't yet begun, but we still see a little of both. Thunderstorms still occur in September, but so does snow. October offers some of the most pleasant weather of the entire year, but you'd better have the snow-

blower ready to go just in case! By November, it can feel like January if subzero air settles in after a big, early snow. Autumn, of all the seasons, seems to have the biggest identity crisis.

As the days grow shorter, we see the end of the thunderstorm season. The lack of intense daytime heating doesn't allow for the strong convective lifting that helps to brew up after-noon storms. Additionally, the mid and upper levels of the atmosphere are comparatively warm after the long summer, so the air is relatively stable. Although the official end of summer is not until the third week of September, for most of us the psychological end of summer is Labor Day weekend. We begin to think less about thunderstorms and more about the first snow of the season.

Usually those early snows first occur in the high country. One morning a thin veil of fresh snow will suddenly show up on the high peaks and usually disappear by midday. Once in a while, an early snow will visit the Front Range cities. The earliest snowstorm on record for Denver was September 3, 1961, when four inches fell over the western suburbs of the city.

DAYS OF AUTUMN

FRONT RANGE
based on Denver

	Sept	Oct	Nov
Average Normal High	77°	67°	53°
Average Normal Low	48°	37°	25°
Record High	97°	90°	79°
Record Low	17°	-2°	-18°
Average Precipitation	1.3"	1.0"	0.9"

HIGH COUNTRY
based on Aspen

	Sept	Oct	Nov
Average Normal High	71°	60°	45°
Average Normal Low	36°	28°	16°
Record High	89°	77°	69°
Record Low	15°	-1°	-19°
Average Precipitation	1.6"	1.5"	1.5"

WESTERN SLOPE
based on Grand Junction

	Sept	Oct	Nov
Average Normal High	81°	67°	51°
Average Normal Low	53°	42°	29°
Record High	100°	88°	75°
Record Low	29°	18°	-2°
Average Precipitation	0.9"	0.9"	0.7"

S. COLORADO
based on Alamosa

	Sept	Oct	Nov
Average Normal High	73°	63°	47°
Average Normal Low	37°	25°	12°
Record High	87°	81°	71°
Record Low	15°	-9°	-30°
Average Precipitation	0.8"	0.6"	0.4"

Source: National Weather Service.
Degrees are in Fahrenheit. Results based on data collected 1961–1990.

Finding Colorado Gold

Nothing says "autumn" in Colorado quite like the sight of a mountainside covered in the stunning leafy gold of aspen trees. Colorado's famous high-country aspen reliably turn gold from the second week of September through the first week of October. *Populus tremuloides*, or the quaking aspen, can be found in all eleven of Colorado's national forests, and their autumn fireworks summon tourists from all across the nation.

Aspen naturally propagate in areas where hardier trees have been damaged or destroyed. This was the case in Colorado, where the slender trees grew in after logging stripped trees from mountain areas. Characterized by their elaborate root systems, aspen reproduce by sending up suckers from the roots to create "clone" stands of trees. These clones, connected underground at the root, are genetically identical to the mother tree. The identical nature of a clone stand is most obvious in spring, when each tree in the stand leafs at the same time, and in fall, when each tree turns the same shade of gold.

Historically, native tribes used aspen bark to make medicinal teas to alleviate fever. The inner bark was sometimes eaten raw in the spring, and the outer bark occasionally produces a powder that was used as a sunscreen. Aspen is a favorite of Colorado wildlife, too. Beaver use aspen for food and building; elk, moose, and deer eat the twigs and foliage. Other names for quaking aspen are golden aspen, mountain aspen, popple, poplar, and trembling poplar.

Despite Coloradans' affinity for aspen, these delicate trees are not recommended for residential landscaping, especially on the plains. Aspen are susceptible to many diseases, their convoluted root systems often grow into sewage drainage systems, and they generally last no longer than about 10 years out of their native habitat.

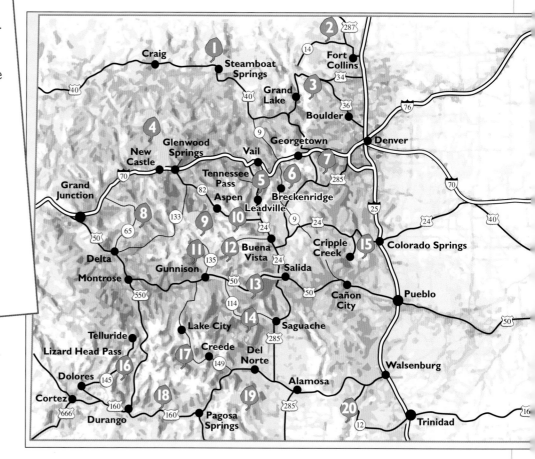

Just a few years ago, on September 21, 1995, Denver was bombed by a record snowfall of nearly ten inches. This soggy, slushy preview of the upcoming season was very unwelcome—it damaged thousands of trees and power lines. The wet, heavy snow settled on trees still covered with leaves, and the overloaded branches crashed down on nearby wires. But even a major storm such as this does not last long in September. Within a day or so, the snow had disappeared under the steady gaze of the warm, early-fall sun. Golfers and gardeners were quickly back on the job under a brilliant blue sky.

Autumn, of all the seasons, seems to have the biggest identity crisis.

Brilliant Aspen Color

Perhaps the most appealing part of autumn is the gold found in the mountains each year. Not the gold sought by prospectors a century ago, but rather the gilded glory of Colorado's famous aspen trees. The decrease in sunlight switches off the mechanism in the leaves that creates chlorophyll—the green color in the leaf. As the green fades, the gold color dominates until the dying leaf flutters to the ground. The best years for aspen viewing are those with well-timed rains and no major fall storms. A too dry summer will send the leaves falling quickly, while a wet summer tends to make them darken to brown or black. The most brilliant display of aspen color occurs when we have a mild, late summer and periodic rain, combined with a dry September that includes few big wind-storms or early snows.

Usually the first signs of aspen gold begin in late August over the higher forests of central Colorado. By the second and third week of September, many aspen groves are well worth a day's drive. Usually the peak time to view aspen is around the last weekend of September. After that, early

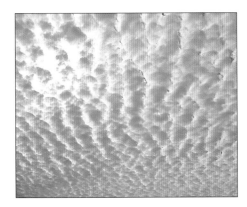

snows may knock down some leaves and others just drop away by themselves. Aspen color does not vary like the shades of red and purple leaves in the Midwest and East, but there is something about gold leaves against a backdrop of rich evergreen and deep blue sky that makes our fall mountains very special indeed.

The First Snow

By mid to late September, the jet-stream winds are beginning to flex their muscles once again. The jet stream usually gets pretty quiet in late summer as the strongest winds aloft are found in central Canada in late July through August. In September, the increasing chill over the northern latitudes helps to force the jet stream farther south once more. As the winds aloft increase over the Rockies, the potential for stronger storm systems and major fluctuations in temperature increases as well. Cold fronts start to roll down from the north with more vigor, and the result can often be a gorgeous summer-like day with a few inches of snow coming right on its heels.

The average date for the first frost in Denver is October 7, with the first measurable snow on October 19. Most years stay snow-free in Denver through September, but October is a different story. In October the first significant low-pressure storm systems of the season begin to form over Colorado. These storms bring easterly upslope winds along the Front Range and often the first opportunity for shovels and snow tires.

October 1997 was memorable for having the biggest snowstorm to hit the eastern plains in fifteen years. A strong jet-stream wind swept a low-pressure system down from the Seattle area on October 23. This low had produced strong winds and rain on the West Coast, but as it moved toward Colorado, two other factors began to come together. To the north, chilly air from Canada was spilling down through the Dakotas. To the south, a warm, moist air mass drifted northward from the Gulf of Mexico. As the low-pressure system spun through the mountains of Colorado, the low became disorganized as it crossed the rugged terrain. Moderate snows fell in the high country, but nothing substantial.

By the night of October 24, however, the low was beginning to exit the mountains and spin off over southern Colorado. At the same time, the chilly air from the north and the muggy southern air were entering Colorado from opposite ends. The stage was set for a major storm! By the morning of October 25, all the ingredients—moisture from the Gulf of Mexico, cold air from Canada, and a re-intensifying storm system over southeast Colorado—swirled into a major storm system. As this mixture spun up, very heavy snow began to fall over the Front Range and northeastern plains. To the southeast, a cold rain covered areas from Colorado Springs to the Oklahoma Panhandle. The low continued to deepen, the winds to strengthen, and soon a full-blown high plains blizzard was in progress.

The storm system slowly churned to the northeast and brought in its wake very cold air howling down from Wyoming. As the snow continued to pile up in northeast Colorado, the rain changed to snow in the southeast—a deadly combination for ranchers on the plains. In the north, farmers and ranchers had to contend with huge drifts and subzero windchills. But in the south, the rain had wetted down most of the cattle, which was then followed by snow and

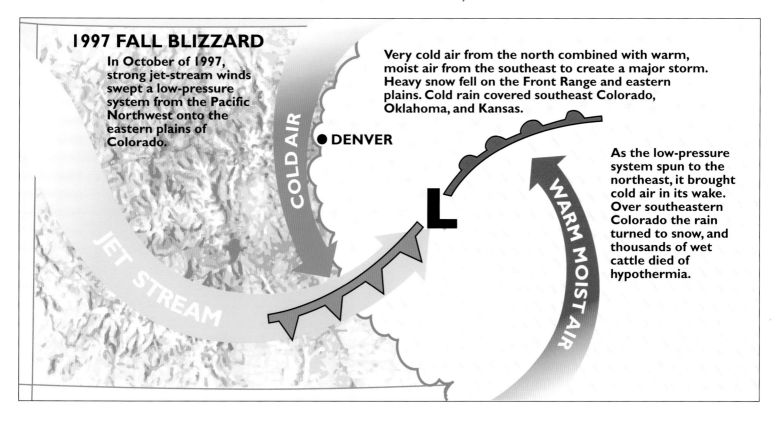

1997 FALL BLIZZARD

In October of 1997, strong jet-stream winds swept a low-pressure system from the Pacific Northwest onto the eastern plains of Colorado.

Very cold air from the north combined with warm, moist air from the southeast to create a major storm. Heavy snow fell on the Front Range and eastern plains. Cold rain covered southeast Colorado, Oklahoma, and Kansas.

● DENVER

COLD AIR

JET STREAM

WARM MOIST AIR

L

As the low-pressure system spun to the northeast, it brought cold air in its wake. Over southeastern Colorado the rain turned to snow, and thousands of wet cattle died of hypothermia.

Fishing in Colorado: Uncle Milty Explains It All

An unofficial landmark on South Broadway, Uncle Milty's Tackle Box has served the Denver area's angling needs for over 30 years. Milton Poffel, Jr., a.k.a. "Uncle Milty," is an aficionado who dispenses wisdom on the vagaries of fishing in Colorado as easily as he dispenses lines, lures, and nightcrawlers.

On ice fishing, for instance: "I honestly believe that fish feel pressure changes in the weather," Uncle Milty says, which is why an overcast winter day is best for hauling out the old rod and reel. "On a bright day, the sun hits the ice, and it cracks and breaks up. The fish feel that and it makes them nervous. Under those conditions, they're looking for cover instead of food."

Then again, according to Uncle Milty, fish are more lethargic in winter and summer, which is why he and most fishermen prefer to fish in fall and spring. In fall, the water cools to 45 or 50 degrees, creating optimum conditions for catching trout. In spring, fish become more active because the water is warmer and contains more oxygen once the ice melts.

"Walleye begin to spawn near shore the day the ice comes off, and ice usually comes off the lakes in March," Uncle Milty notes. Colorado's unpredictable climate can also affect fishing, though. "I've fished Lake Granby at the end of May, and it's been frozen solid. The weather patterns have a lot to do with it. But once the thaw starts, it goes fast." Did El Niño bother the fish? "I don't think it affected fishing in Colorado one bit," he says. "But it did affect my business. The weather stayed cooler, and people waited longer before coming in to buy fishing equipment."

Uncle Milty has been fishing in Colorado since he moved west over 40 years ago, so when he suggests using mealworms, wax worms, and maggots for winter bait and night crawlers, spinners, lures, and flies for summer bait, Coloradans listen.

Uncle Milty's Nine Fishing Tips

1. You'll find rainbow trout in lakes at depths of 12 to 15 feet at any time of year.

2. Catch brown trout in autumn, when they are spawning and the cooler water temperatures make them more active.

3. Craving mackinaw in spring? Mackinaw season at Blue Mesa Reservoir outside of Gunnison begins as soon as the water warms up. "The ice comes off Blue Mesa in a fury, and when it does, it makes the mackinaw happy, and they come into the shallow water," Uncle Milty notes.

4. Depth perception: in summer you'll find bass at 5 feet deep, walleye at 25 feet deep, pike at 5 feet deep, and catfish at 10 feet deep.

5. Brave the elements: fish when it's windy and rainy. The wind blows insects and small wildlife into the water, which attracts porridge fish and crustaceans and brings larger fish close to shore. Uncle Milty instructs, "Put on a poncho and fish in the storm."

6. Then again, never, ever fish in a lightning storm. "I was fishing in Wyoming, lightning hit across the river from me, and my fishing rod started snapping and popping," Uncle Milty relates.

7. Top spot for fall fishing: Chatfield Reservoir. The trout are plentiful, and you'll have practically no competition for it.

8. Bad luck fishing? Maybe it's your aftershave. "Fish are wary of strong scents," Uncle Milty contends, so leave the perfume, cologne, cigarettes, and cigars at home.

9. Finally, if your luck's been really bad and you're desperate to catch any fish at all, fish on a clear night during a full moon.

sharply colder temperatures, bringing the threat of hypothermia. Tens of thousands of cattle died during the storm—the worst loss in years for Colorado ranchers.

In Denver, snow piled up two and three feet deep, the worst blizzard since the infamous Christmas of '82 storm. Streets and highways were impassable, and Denver International Airport was closed for hours as crews literally could not get to the airport. The Denver Broncos nearly missed their flight to Buffalo—ironically, Buffalo, typically a city with a lot of snow, was sunny and mild at the time. By the morning of October 26, the storm had cleared out. Although sunshine followed, it took several days to melt down the deep drifts—and many Halloween trick-or-treaters went out the door with a pair of snow boots!

Indian Summer

Autumn is not just a waiting period for the inevitable onslaught of winter. Every Coloradan looks forward to the delightful stretch of warm, sunny days known as "Indian summer"—perhaps the nicest weather of the entire year. Brilliant blue skies, highs in the perfectly comfortable seventy-degree range, light breezes — in other words, ideal! Indian summer is loosely defined as the warm, dry, quiet period of weather that follows the first killing frost. This weather pattern usually occurs during late September or the first two weeks of October, and is especially delightful because it coincides with the peak of the aspen leaves. There really is no meteorological significance to Indian summer — it doesn't portend anything about the upcoming winter or reflect on the summer just past. Indian summer is simply a time to try to slow down and savor the good fortune of living in Colorado.

The First Cold Front

As the days of Indian summer drift along, keep an eye on the television weather map. Inevitably a cold front will appear over central Canada. This front will usher in the first cold snap of winter. As the days grow shorter here, they are really getting short in northern Canada. Daylight dwindles down to just a few precious hours, and even that is with a faint sun that is low on the horizon. Warmth is escaping from the atmosphere over the northern latitudes much faster than it is being replenished. As snow begins to fall over Canada, the ground temperatures struggle to stay near freezing, but they soon give up and head toward zero or colder. The cold air becomes a dense, stable air mass that slowly grows over the thin spruce forests and tundra of northern Canada and Alaska. The sheer weight of the cold, dense air creates a high-pressure area over the region. If you've ever had a flat tire, you know that air flows from high pressure (inside the tire) toward lower pressure (outside the tire). As the high builds in Canada, the pressure difference becomes large enough to begin to push southward toward the United States. The leading edge of this cold mass of high pressure is one of those blue pointed lines on the weather map — the cold front!

The Routt Divide Blowdown: A Blast of Nature.
Could it happen again?

For over twelve hours on October 25, 1997, fiercely strong winds blew from the east over the Continental Divide often in excess of 120 miles per hour. The result?

A path of devastation almost five miles wide and thirty miles long that flattened over four million spruce and fir trees in the Routt National Forest, located in the northwest sector of Colorado.

So what happened? According to Greg Poulos of Colorado Research Associates in Boulder, the blowdown was produced by an unusual wind reversal. Winds in Colorado typically flow west to east, but on that day in 1997, strong winds raged westward instead. "One of the reasons the blowdown occurred was the unusual strength and depth of the easterly flow from the cutoff low-pressure system," says Poulos. Coloradans will remember that the same low-pressure system ushered in a sudden blizzard to the Front Range on October 24 and effectively shut down much of the city and Denver International Airport.

The Routt Blowdown occurred deep in the forest, so there were few human witnesses. Meteorologists have hypothesized the causes and effects of the event by utilizing the RAMS computer model to simulate the conditions of October 25, 1997. RAMS, which stands for Regional Atmospheric Modeling System, was developed at Colorado State University in Fort Collins.

The U.S. Forest Service states that the Routt area will slowly recuperate over the next few decades, but Coloradans want to know: Could such devastation happen in populated areas like Conifer or Evergreen? Possibly, say meteorologists, but worried mountain dwellers are advised to regard such a phenomenon in terms of a 100-year flood; according to scientist John Snook, "There's always a one percent chance of a 100-year flood happening." In other words, file a repeat of the Routt Divide Blowdown under "possible, but not likely" in the annals of bizarre weather in Colorado.

For more information on the Routt Divide Blowdown, contact the Medicine Bow–Routt National Forest at (970) 879-1870 or call the Blowdown Hotline at (970) 870-2192. Remember, the Routt Divide Blowdown area (which includes the Rabbit Ears Pass and Buffalo Pass regions) still contains serious hazards to public safety as additional trees may fall, and recreational access may be limited. Be sure to call ahead.

As this front sags southward, the first icy details of the cold wave make the television news. "Low temperatures in North Dakota and Montana dipped below zero early today," we say with a grim smile. Ahead of the front, the weather may be warm and sunny with little sign of impending trouble. But watch the skies for signs of wispy cirrus clouds to the north. There won't be many, but even a few may offer a clue. A home barometer may signal a change in the weather as it will gradually fall ahead of

the approaching front. Winds may shift from southwesterly to light from the southeast. Don't feel bad if you miss the subtle symptoms of this weather change—the approach of a Canadian cold front is not well marked. The passage of such a front, however, is a different story.

As the icy air pours down across Wyoming, the sky to our north will darken and billowy clouds will gather. Chances are good those clouds are not just full of moisture, but also swirling dust from the plains to the north. When the cold front roars down the Front Range, winds will abruptly switch to the north and whip up to forty miles per hour or more. Clouds will rapidly lower, dust and tumbleweeds will sweep by, and then the snow will fall. This type of front may push from the Wyoming border to northern New Mexico in three or four hours. Snow will fall for several hours after the front passes and may pile up to four to six inches in a hurry. After that the skies clear and the center of the cold high-pressure area settles in for a couple of days. By November, it's not uncommon for such a weather-maker to bring temperatures down to the single digits. An interesting fact is that these weather fronts are responsible for the term "blizzard," which is a derivative of the German word for lightning. Early European settlers on the high plains were astounded by the lightning-fast changes in the weather, especially when a powerful cold front roared through.

Like spring, autumn is a transition season. It offers the nicest weather of the year— warm, gentle days with the beauty of blue sky and golden leaves. By the end of the season, however, autumn leaves us with wind, cold, and snow aplenty— preparing us for the white wonderland of winter.

Colorado WINTER

O f all the seasons of the year, winter is the one that most people around the country would identify with Colorado. Our high elevation means that it is winter for most of the year on our mountain peaks, with the snow-free time lasting only a few weeks.

The winter season often begins well ahead of the calendar, as the first snows in Denver often come as early as mid-September. Newscasts from around the nation show us digging out of the deep drifts well before Halloween. Yet the big secret that we keep is that we are not left snowbound for months by these big storms. Instead, the rest of the country stops paying attention to us while the snow quickly melts, and we're out playing golf again by the end of the week!

Winter in Colorado is not just about snowing, but also blowing! Powerful chinook winds often roar down the mountains onto the plains. Gusts may exceed 100 miles per hour in places like Boulder and Golden. These warm, dry winds can quickly pull us out of a deep freeze and put our temperatures into the fifties and sixties in a matter of hours. The low humidity these winds carry mean they can make fast work out of a pile of snow. The word "chinook" is a Native American term meaning "snow-eater."

Colorado serves as a breeding ground for some of the most powerful storm systems that bomb the rest of the central and eastern United States with heavy snow. Low-pressure storm systems frequently develop just to the east or to

DAYS OF WINTER

FRONT RANGE
based on Denver

	Dec	Jan	Feb
Average Normal High	45°	43°	47°
Average Normal Low	17°	16°	20°
Record High	79°	76°	77°
Record Low	−25°	−29°	−25°
Average Precipitation	0.6"	0.5"	0.6"

HIGH COUNTRY
based on Aspen*

	Dec	Jan	Feb
Average Normal High	37°	34°	37°
Average Normal Low	9°	6°	8°
Record High	62°	58°	60°
Record Low	−21°	−37°	−30°
Average Precipitation	1.7"	1.8"	1.6"

WESTERN SLOPE
based on Grand Junction

	Dec	Jan	Feb
Average Normal High	39°	36°	45°
Average Normal Low	19°	15°	24°
Record High	66°	62°	70°
Record Low	−21°	−23°	−21°
Average Precipitation	0.6"	0.6"	0.5"

S. COLORADO
based on Alamosa

	Dec	Jan	Feb
Average Normal High	35°	33°	40°
Average Normal Low	−1°	−4°	5°
Record High	61°	62°	66°
Record Low	−42°	−50°	−35°
Average Precipitation	0.4"	0.3"	0.3"

Source: National Weather Service.
Degrees are in Fahrenheit. Results based on data collected 1961–1990.
*Source: International Station Meteorological Climate Summary, version 4.0

the "lee" of the Rockies. Strong winds aloft at the jet-stream level (about 25,000–30,000 feet) squeeze over the mountain peaks and then over the plains. As the air moves out away from the mountains, the pressure falls, creating a low-pressure area. If conditions are right, this low will begin to swirl moisture into the region from the Gulf of Mexico. This moisture spins into clouds, rain, and snow and before long, a storm is born. These storm systems first dump heavy snow over eastern Colorado and then churn to the northeast. Heavy, wet snow, sleet, freezing rain, and even thunderstorms mark the path of these storms as they roll on toward the Great Lakes. The soggy storm systems that spin out of eastern Colorado can give a false impression to the rest of the nation. Those eastern storms often dump heavy snow on Denver, Colorado

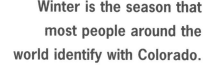

Winter is the season that most people around the world identify with Colorado.

Springs, Limon, or other cities on the plains but leave the mountains with a much smaller accumulation. Television weather reports around the country will show all the snow in Denver, and the folks in other cities figure, "If Denver has a foot of snow, the mountains must really have been hammered!" In fact, eastern storms tend to be

blocked off by the mountains of the Front Range, and the ski areas may have only scattered clouds while Denver gets a foot of snow. This was the case in October 1984, when the Broncos and the Packers played in a blizzard at Mile High Stadium. The national television audience saw all that snow in Denver and inundated the ski resorts with calls for reservations. Being good businesspeople, ski resort personnel didn't mention the fact that at the time, skies were clear in Vail and Aspen!

An old saying about Colorado weather is very helpful when trying to figure out if a storm system will bring heavy snow. Remember—Pacific front, mountains bear the brunt; southeast low, Denver gets the snow. As discussed earlier, storm systems on the eastern plains spin their heavy snow over the Front Range and adjacent plains, but may miss the mountains. In contrast, a moist storm front from the Pacific Coast may dump very heavy snow on the mountains, but

Snowboarding: A Colorado Passion

Embarrassed by your first attempt to snowboard in the high country? Did you spend more time with your face in the snow than with your feet on the board? Don't let it get you down, says former International Snowboarding Federation overall world champion Kevin Delaney. "My first experience with a snowboard was kind of lame," he admits. "I fell down a lot. But my first turn was it. I could feel the powder spraying up and feel all of the terrain."

Initially a hockey player, skier, and skateboarder, Delaney became a passionate convert to snowboarding in 1980. Twelve years later, Delaney founded Delaney Snowboarding with his brother Brian, 1990 NCAA and National Amateur Snowboarding Champion. The Delaneys have dedicated themselves to promoting the sport, and the snowboarding camps Delaney Snowboarding offers at Copper Mountain Resort in Colorado and Mammoth Mountain Resort in California were born of that dedication.

According to the snowboarding industry, only 28 percent of the skiing population snowboards, though the number increases each season. "Snowboarding is easier to learn than skiing, but a lot of people haven't tried it yet," Delaney notes, citing not only the sport's perceived dangers, but also its reputation as the extreme preoccupation of young, out-of-control "shredders" tearing down the slopes. Delaney will tell you that the average age of the snowboarder is increasing and notes that instead of "bashing this growth sport, the skiing industry is now embracing it."

Delaney's primary caution to snowboarders of all skill levels is to stay in the boundaries set by the resort. Snowboarding out of bounds is especially hazardous in spring when the avalanche danger is high. But snowboarding in March and April is worth it — the days are longer and warmer, the accommodations and lift tickets are cheaper, and the atmosphere is relaxed. "There's a party mood on the mountain in spring," Delaney says, "and piles and piles of snow."

Kevin Delaney's Top Nine Snowboarding Tips

1. Prepare for any kind of weather any time of year. Winter's hazards are obvious, but spring weather brings its own set of problems. Freak rain showers and a greater threat of avalanche punctuate springtime in the Rockies. Delaney adds: "There's also 75 percent fewer people around to notice you if something goes wrong."

2. Stay in good physical shape. As the season progresses, the snow will get heavier and wetter, which makes moving your snowboard more of a challenge.

3. Protect your eyes. Along with adequate layered clothing, a coat, hat, and gloves, take along a pair of goggles. Goggles prevent snow blindness, which can permanently damage the eye's retina. Each snow crystal has multiple facets, and as Delaney notes, "one of them is always shining like a mirror and reflecting into your eye."

4. Use sunscreen, even if it's cloudy. "Harmful rays will punch through the clouds," Delaney warns.

5. Stay hydrated. Drink lots of water and carry nutritional bars with you.

6. Tune your snowboard regularly. Snowboarders can get stuck in the flats with the wrong wax. Switch to a warmer wax in April to accommodate the heavier spring snow.

7. Be light on your feet. Hidden rocks, trees, or stumps can damage your board. Going from shady to sunny areas might catch you off guard as snow conditions change.

8. Concentrate on keeping your weight centered over your snowboard—balance is everything. And be prepared for surprises. "If you go from a shady area to a sunny area, your wax is wrong, and you're caught off guard, you'll get ejected over the handlebars," says Delaney.

9. Stay for the apres-ski party! Don a Hawaiian shirt and be the life of the party. Snowboarding is a social sport, too!

have little moisture remaining by the time the storm slips down into Denver. Those Pacific fronts have a rough time staying intact as they first hit the Cascades and Sierra Nevada mountains, then have to cross the Wasatch Range in Utah and finally struggle over the Continental Divide. When the once mighty storm finally tops the last of three or four mountain ranges, moisture is so depleted that Denver doesn't get even a flake of snow.

DEEP-FREEZE CONDITIONS

Light winds and clear skies allow solar energy, reflected off the snowpack, to escape into space through the thin mountain air.

Heavier, cold air flows down the mountainsides and pools in the mountain valleys, maintaining frigid temperatures.

Frigid Temperatures

Winter is a season of extreme deep freeze conditions over the state. The coldest reading on record for Colorado is –61 degrees at Maybell on February 2, 1985. Our high mountain valleys tend to be the chilly spots as the thin mountain air allows the heat of the day to rapidly escape into space after sunset. The cold, dense air then begins to pool in the valley, leaving the mountainsides a bit milder. Gunnison, Alamosa, Taylor Park, Fairplay, and Fraser all plummet to readings of 40 to 50 below at times during January and February. The best combination for extreme cold is a deep snowpack, clear skies, and light winds.

Winter Winds

One of the less attractive but still important aspects of winter weather is the infamous "brown cloud." This unwelcome phenomenon is a direct result of population growth along the Front Range. Trains, planes, and automobiles, along with industry and home fireplaces, release billions of tiny particles into the air. These minute bits of air pollution swirl around the Front Range on a daily basis, but under certain weather conditions, they are trapped over the metro area and build up over a period of days. The best (or worse) scenario for the brown cloud is a combination of light winds aloft and cold temperatures at the surface, which is called an inversion. Under these circumstances, the cold air at ground level is heavy and stable, minimizing mixing of the air. The light winds aloft mean little change will occur in

the overall pattern, and no major weather fronts are on the way. Day after day the air fills with more and more pollution—and the brownish cloud grows thicker.

It is interesting to note that the brown cloud is nothing new. Native Americans told the early pioneers about a brown cloud that developed from their campfires during the cold season! Indeed, there are times when the brown cloud can develop even with very strong winds over the mountains. In this case, the winds roar over the mountain peaks and then drop down just east of Denver. Limon, Fort Morgan, and Greeley may have very strong westerly winds while Denver and its vicinity are caught in a light easterly "backwash" of air and remain with a sluggish brown cloud pattern. Every other town has people holding onto their hats!

Certain weather patterns can leave Colorado with a very wide range of conditions at the same time. Strong jet-stream winds may slam into the mountains, bringing strong wind and snow to the high country. Those same winds are forced up and over the peaks and then blow down toward Denver as a warm, dry Chinook. Boulder and the Fort Collins

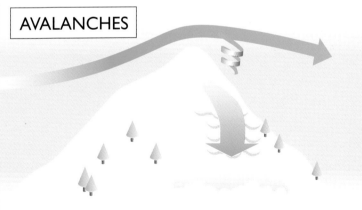

DANGEROUS WINTER WINDS

INVERSIONS

Light winds of warm air flow above a stable mass of heavier cold air, acting like a lid over the Front Range. Pollutants are trapped and accumulate to create the "Brown Cloud."

The Brown Cloud

TURBULENT WINDS

Lenticular Cloud

Rotor Cloud

Chinook Winds

Turbulent winds are created as the jet stream collides with Colorado's mountain peaks. The deflected winds sculpt beautiful lenticular clouds above the mountains. Strong winds roaring down the mountains can create a dangerous rolling mass of air, indicated by rotor clouds. These winds, known as Chinooks, can create very gusty conditions on the eastern plains.

AVALANCHES

Swirling eddies are created in the wind as it passes over mountain peaks. These pack the snow into large, unstable cornices, which can eventually give way and slide downhill, triggering an avalanche.

Damage from Chinook winds.

area "batten down" for a strong blast of wind, but the air currents bounce back up higher in the skies over Denver. Thus the cities of Denver and Aurora are left with light winds and bad air. Meanwhile, the air currents return to the surface east of Denver and bring gusty conditions to the eastern plains, under mostly clear skies. Thus snowing, blowing, bad air, and clear skies can all come from just one weather feature—all thanks to the topography of Colorado!

Fascinating cloud formations are a frequent sight in our winter skies. Strong winds blowing over the mountains can create the lenticular or "flying saucer" clouds, described earlier. These clouds occur at mid-levels of the troposphere (about 20,000 feet above sea level), and are especially beautiful in the evening and early morning, when the low angle of the sun casts a haunting gold and reddish hue to these unusual clouds.

The official meteorological name for flying saucer clouds is a real mouthful—"altocumulus standing lenticularus." This long

Lenticular clouds

moniker is often shortened by weather forecasters to just "ACSL." Lenticular clouds are a good indicator of a developing chinook wind event along the Front Range. Since they are created by strong western winds aloft, it follows that some of that momentum will sweep down the eastern flanks of the Rockies and blow into chinook-prone places like Boulder and northern Jefferson County. The appearance of lenticulars can also be a harbinger of an approaching snowstorm. The jet-stream winds that first create the ACSL clouds can then aid in the development of a strong low-pressure system over Colorado. So remember, when you see those flying saucer clouds, be ready for some changes in the weather—maybe some BIG changes!

Another aspect of strong winds along the Front Range is the "rotor clouds." These clouds are just what their name implies—a rotating cloud—but they are not tornadoes. The tornado rotates on a vertical axis, but a rotor cloud spins like a pencil rolling off a desk. Go back to the analogy of the mountain stream. In certain areas, the water motion could develop into a standing rapid that has the water swirling over and over on itself. If you have been

whitewater rafting, this is one thing the guides warn you about! Winds descend from the mountaintops and may develop into a swirling band about halfway down from the top. Any moisture in this swirl of air will form into a cloud that rolls over and over, while staying at about the same location on the mountainside. Rotor clouds are of special concern to pilots as the descending air currents can trap a helicopter or aircraft into a deadly fall—even at full power. Wintertime pilots are especially wary of rotors, and watch lenticulars very carefully as the same conditions can create the rotor clouds.

Avalanche!

One of the most awesome winter sights in Colorado is an avalanche. Strong storms may pile two to three feet of snow on the peaks in just a matter of a day or two. This snow surface may be very unstable for a variety of reasons. The sheer weight of the fresh snow may cause numerous slides in the first few hours after a major storm. This is especially true on slopes greater than thirty degrees. However, strong winds that usually accompany a snowstorm can pack the snow into drifts and cornices that can suddenly break free and race downhill. As the snowslide thunders down, it gathers momentum and

Unstable, wind-packed cornices and snow drifts.

volume and can become hundreds of feet wide. Look carefully at mountain forest patterns and you will see the effects of snowslides—they can instantly clear thousands of trees from the side of a mountain. In fact, Loveland Ski Area unexpectedly got a brand-new expert run a couple of years ago as a slide roared right into the parking lot. It took out a few cars, but also cleared the trees for a new run.

Avalanches are one of our biggest threats during the winter season. Every year backcountry skiers are trapped in snowslides, and every year there are fatalities. The snow that an avalanche packs in can have the weight and consistency of wet cement. A skier caught under even a foot of snow may not be able to move at all. This is especially

The Power of a Powder Avalanche

Colorado experiences an average of 20,000 avalanches per year, a small percentage of which affect the state's human population. About 60 people are caught each year in avalanches, with approximately six deaths. Economic losses can be substantial. Direct property damage averages about $100,000 per year, although indirect losses can be as high as $3–5 million. (For example, a big snowstorm on a weekend could cause an avalanche that might close a highway, preventing 10,000 skiers from reaching ski resorts and resulting in a weekend revenue loss of as much as $500,000.)

Avalanche Hotlines

The following phone numbers, updated daily during avalanche season by the Colorado Avalanche Information Center, will provide you with the most recent information on local weather, snow, and avalanche conditions.

Colorado Springs
(719) 520-0020

Denver
(303) 275-5360

Durango	(970) 247-8187
Fort Collins	(970) 482-0457
Summit County	(970) 668-0600

U.S. Forest Service/Aspen
(970) 920-1664

U.S. Forest Service/Vail
(970) 827-5687

Snow in an avalanche can have the weight and consistency of wet cement.

true of the so called "slab" avalanches that occur when old, compacted snow breaks off in large chunks or slabs and comes crashing down the mountainside. Skiing in the backcountry can be a beautiful, serene experience, but it can also be a deadly one for those unfamiliar with avalanche structure and avalanche safety. Be sure you know what you are doing before risking your life or the lives of those who may have to rescue you.

Students identify layers in a cross-section of a slab of snow. Weak, underlying layers can give way, allowing the slab to slide downhill and create an avalanche.

Knox Williams's Top Nine Ways To Avoid Avalanches

Colorado's high country, known the world over for its awe-inspiring majesty, is also honored as the Unofficial Avalanche Capital of the U.S. Over 20,000 avalanches occur in Colorado each year. These snow-slides range from the barely significant (when small amounts of snow travel at 30 miles per hour) to the huge and deadly, when entire chunks of a mountainside roar downward at speeds up to 100 miles per hour. While other western mountain ranges also experience snowslides each season, the Colorado Rockies are especially avalanche-prone because the snowpack tends to be shallower and colder. A Colorado mountainside is also more likely to meet all four of the criteria necessary for snowslides, as it will have 1) a slope of 25 to 50 degrees, 2) a slab of snow, 3) an unstable, weak layer underlying the slab, and 4) a trigger—an additional load of new snow, or an animal, a person, or explosion that disrupts the tenuous balance in the terrain.

The best way to avoid an avalanche is to simply avoid avalanche terrain. If you must travel in the backcountry, where most avalanches happen, keep in mind these nine tips compiled by Knox Williams of the Colorado Avalanche Information Center:

1. Stay alert to conditions. Before leaving home, check weather and avalanche reports.

2. Be patient. Wait and watch the terrain from protected areas.

3. Equip yourself. Carry a slope meter, beacons, shovels, and collapsible probes. This equipment can be purchased at outdoor recreation outfitters.

4. Choose your companions wisely. Travel with skilled people experienced in the backcountry, and stay in sight of each other at all times.

5. Read the terrain. The safest routes are broad valleys, ridge tops, or windward sides of ridges. Avoid narrow valleys, cornices, and lee slopes.

6. Note the slope. Lower-angle slopes are safer than steeper slopes. Gentle slopes may be overrun by avalanches releasing on steep slopes above.

7. Step lightly. Cross, climb, or descend suspect slopes one person at a time. Cross each slope as high as possible.

8. Look for protection. Keep to the edges of open slopes and gullies. Use ridges, rock outcrops, and dense timber as a possible refuge.

9. Use your head. Minimize the time you are exposed to danger. Stop to eat, rest, or camp in avalanche-free zones.

OK, so you've taken all the precautions, but here comes the snow. What do you do now? If you are the one caught in the avalanche:

- Escape to the side and try to grab a tree.
- If possible, ditch heavy packs, poles, and skis. If you're on a snowmobile, get clear of it as quickly as possible.
- Fight the avalanche by "swimming" through the snow.
- Form an air pocket around your face with your hands before the snow stops.

If you are the one in a rescuer role:
- Begin by searching downslope from the last place you saw the victim.
- If you have probes with you, begin probing for the victim in the immediate area, and then branch out into likely areas.
- Do not go for help prematurely. Stay on-site for as long as possible—victims have a better chance of survival if you are able to locate and rescue them quickly.
- Be ready to treat any victim for suffocation, impact injuries, shock, and hypothermia.

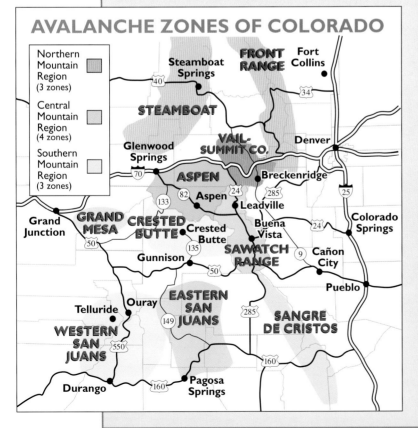

AVALANCHE ZONES OF COLORADO

- Northern Mountain Region (3 zones)
- Central Mountain Region (4 zones)
- Southern Mountain Region (3 zones)

Steamboat Springs
FRONT RANGE
Fort Collins
STEAMBOAT
VAIL-SUMMIT CO.
Glenwood Springs
Denver
ASPEN
Breckenridge
Aspen
Leadville
Grand Junction
GRAND MESA
CRESTED BUTTE
Crested Butte
Buena Vista
Colorado Springs
Gunnison
SAWATCH RANGE
Cañon City
Pueblo
Telluride
Ouray
EASTERN SAN JUANS
SANGRE DE CRISTOS
WESTERN SAN JUANS
Durango
Pagosa Springs

Blizzards

The only kind of avalanche the city of Denver ever experiences is when we watch the Colorado Avalanche play hockey, but we still can get plenty of snowy excitement from good old high plains blizzards. The true definition of a blizzard has more to do with wind and visibility than snow—a storm earns blizzard status when winds of thirty-five miles per hour or higher are accompanied by falling or blowing snow that drops visibility to a quarter mile or less. The sky above can be clear, but blowing snow at ground level can produce blizzard conditions. A severe blizzard is bad—winds over fifty miles per hour with visibility near zero due to blowing or falling snow. Certainly our pioneer ancestors saw some very scary winter storms, but even today strong winter storms can bring peril to travelers. The wide-open eastern plains of Colorado offer no resistance to the wind and can allow howling storms to swirl snow into drifts five to ten feet high during the worst blizzards.

If you drive along the road to Denver International Airport, or many other highways in open country, you may wonder about the big snow fences. These large wooden structures help keep the roads free of blowing and drifting snow. The snow fence works by causing the wind to blow up and over the wooden structure. When this happens, the speed of the wind drops slightly. This reduces the amount of snow that can be carried by the wind, and allows the snow to fall out

A snow fence

of the air and pile up near the snow fence. Careful placement of these fences keeps the big drifts off the roads—hopefully!

We're fortunate in Colorado because our winter snows offer a wealth of recreational activities to keep us busy through the cold season. In addition, thanks to our mostly dry and sunny climate, we are seldom faced with the bleak grayness of the long winters in the Midwest or the Northeast. The lovely stretches of mild and clear weather are punctuated by brief periods of snow, wind, and cold—instead of the other way around! Before too long, the snows begin to melt away and the cycle of the seasons begins anew over Colorado.

Weather of the CENTURY

Many of the most weatherwise people in the world live right along the Front Range of Colorado. With the combination of the National Center for Atmospheric Research (NCAR) in Boulder, an excellent local National Weather Service office, and the Department of Atmospheric Science at Colorado State University in Fort Collins, to name a few, there's a lot of meteorological horsepower in the area. Part of the reason so many weather experts have settled in this area is the fascinating combination of weather events that we get here. Most weather researchers and historians really love watching storms! Over the past century, there have been dozens of notable events in Colorado weather. In this chapter, with the help of Nolan Doesken, Assistant State Climatologist at Colorado State University in Fort Collins, I'll highlight some of the top weather events in Colorado.

The National Center for Atmospheric Research in Boulder.

Actual weather records date back to around 1870 in Colorado. There are earlier mentions of specific storms or cold waves, but the continuous recording of daily weather extends back about 130 years. In fact, one of the earliest references to Colorado weather is still used today. According to the Colorado Climate Center Library, sometime around 1870, the Colorado Promotion and Publicity Committee came up with the statement that "Colorado has three hundred days of sunshine a year." This comment was picked up by the *New York Independent* and run in their September 26, 1872, issue—and the boast has been around ever since. If you go to various chambers of commerce in the state, you'll still find it! The truth is that this is a bit of a stretch. To come up with three hundred days of sunshine a year, you

An 1887 flood roars through the town of Blackhawk.

57

Zebulon Pike

have to count days that are sunny in the morning and cloudy in the afternoon as well as days when the skies are covered by clouds, but not thick clouds. This will get you into the upper two hundreds, unless you are in a place like Alamosa, which legitimately may be able to claim three hundred and more days of sunshine a year.

The earliest weather references came from journals written by explorers in the first part of the nineteenth century. Lewis and Clark did not venture into what was to become the state of Colorado, but they were instructed by President Thomas Jefferson to make precise readings of temperature and sky conditions along their route. Zebulon Pike continued that tradition in the fall of 1806 as his exploration party attempted to climb the mountain that today bears his name. In his journal, he recorded:

26th November, Wednesday
We had a fine, clear sky, whilst it was snowing at the bottom.

27th November, Thursday
The unbounded prairie was overhung with clouds, which appeared like the ocean in a storm; wave piled on wave and foaming, whilst the sky was perfectly clear where we were. Commenced our march up the mountain, and in about one hour arrived at the summit of this chain: here we found snow middle deep; no sign of beast or bird inhabiting this region. The thermometer which stood at nine degrees above zero at the foot of the mountain, here fell to four degrees below zero.

(from *Georgetown Weather Observations: A Historical Perspective*, William E. Wilson)

Deep snow in Eldora during the 1890s.

What Colonel Pike observed was a classic upslope condition on the eastern plains. Low-level easterly winds had pushed clouds over the plains, while the mountain itself was bathed in sunshine. (That mountain, by the way, was not actually Pikes Peak but rather Cheyenne Mountain. From the top they could see the much higher mountain nearby.)

In 1820, Captain John Bell acted as the official journalist for Stephen H. Long's expedition to the Rockies. On Wednesday, July 5, the party camped on the Platte River near the mouth of a creek in a grove of cottonwood trees "that shaded us from the scorching rays of the altitude of the mercury at ninety-one degrees." The creek they camped on they named Cannon Ball Creek because of the large round stones in its bed. Today we know this tributary as Clear Creek.

Pikes Peak as seen from the Garden of the Gods.

Crested Butte: Turning Snow into Fun and Profit

Winter weather has been not only Crested Butte's greatest asset but also its most bedeviling challenge. The Ute tribes, who first inhabited the area, did so only in summer to establish hunting grounds. By the 1880s when the railroad arrived, keeping the tracks clear became a problem. Locomotives with special snow-clearing equipment attached to the cow-catchers could spend days cutting a path into town. Ironically, when the last coal mine closed in Crested Butte in 1952, the town developed ski areas to exploit the town's one-time winter nemesis—snow.

Crested Butte boasts an elevation of 8,885 feet, while Mount Crested Butte, site of the ski resort, rests at 9,356 feet and accommodates up to 6,500 guests in winter (nearly 1,300 people live in the town year-round). The town is blessed with mild temperatures in summer—and a bountiful 322 inches of snow in winter. A recreationist's paradise any time of year, Crested Butte offers ready access to Lake Irwin, Taylor Reservoir, Blue Mesa Reservoir, Gunnison National Forest, the Maroon Bells, Snowmass, and the Oh-Be-Joyful Wilderness Area. Summer festivals attract tourists from around the country.

If you're in the Crested Butte area, be sure to check out the Rocky Mountain Biological Laboratory (RMBL) in nearby Gothic. Founded in 1928 by Dr. John C. Johnson as a research facility for mountain biology, today the RMBL is known the world over as the nation's foremost high-altitude field station.

Colorado weather records go back to the 1800s.

John C. Fremont made four expeditions into the Rocky Mountains and kept detailed weather observations of temperature, barometric readings, wind, rain, snow, and sky cover. Part of his motivation was to provide accurate data for the construction of railroads. In the winter of 1848–49, Fremont crossed the San Juan Mountains in order to find the best path for a railway. He wanted to see the mountains under the most adverse conditions so that he could determine the safest route. His men faced a terrible ordeal of snow, wind, and bitter cold, and many in the party were lost. In a letter to his wife, Fremont wrote that prior to the onset of the blizzard, "the cold was extraordinary; at the warmest hours of the day (between one and two) the thermometer (Fahrenheit) standing in the shade of only a tree trunk at zero; the day sunshiny with a moderate breeze."

The 1870s opened up vast areas of the West for settlers. J. T. Gardner was a member of several surveying expeditions into the Colorado Rockies. The U.S. Signal Service was responsible for establishing early weather stations in Colorado. These sites all had

substantially different elevations, allowing for comparisons of pressure and temperature. Readings were taken three times daily at approximately 7:00 A.M., 2:00 P.M., and 9:00 P.M. Gardner himself spent two days and a night on the top of Pikes Peak and made the following observations in a letter to his wife: "It snowed and blew bitterly cold, but there were hours of wonderful clearness when I saw points 150 miles off."

Since the 1870s, the observation network has expanded tremendously over Colorado. Literally hundreds of observations pour into the Colorado Climate Center each day. Data comes from sophisticated satellites and radars as well as automated weather stations that provide information on a continuous basis. At 9NEWS, we show the automated data as part of our "School-Net"—a statewide network of weather reporting stations set up at nearly seventy schools across Colorado. School-Net

The Fort Collins Flood of 1997.

is part of a nationwide network of weather stations called the Automated Weather Source (AWS). Over a thousand schools across the United States participate in the AWS program. Many of these schools put their data directly out on the Internet, so the data can be accessed instantly from anywhere in the world—quite a leap in technology from the pioneer days!

Whether the weather is witnessed by human eyes and ears or by an automated station, one thing is for sure—we get plenty of variety in Colorado. You've heard the old saying, "If you don't like the weather, wait five minutes and it will change." Now, everyone loves to brag about their weather, and I've heard this said in Wisconsin, Illinois, and Missouri. But I have to say that in Colorado, you don't even need to wait the five minutes! Our weather can take some amazing dips from warm and dry to bitter cold and snowy and everything else in between.

In that light, with the aid of Nolan Doesken, here is a list of some big Colorado weather stories of the twentieth century.

The Snowstorm of December 2–6, 1913

The entire state felt the effects of the great snowstorm of 1913, when an incredible storm dumped thirty to fifty inches of wet snow from Trinidad to Fort Collins. "Heavy wet snow was followed by heavy windblown snow," Nolan Doesken notes. "The storm paralyzed the

eastern Colorado Front Range corridor from Raton Pass to Cheyenne and on up to the Continental Divide. Longmont should be thankful for this storm because building codes for roofs in the town changed as a result."

Caused by a low-pressure system that swirled in from Arizona on November 30, this system was not much different from many that we get during the course of a Rocky Mountain winter. For the first three days of December, the storm brought light to moderate snows as the low slowly dropped into New Mexico. On December 4, however, the low began to move almost due north over the eastern plains of Colorado, bringing a tremendous easterly upslope flow to the plains and mountains east of the Continental Divide. Heavy rains soaked the far eastern plains, while significant amounts of snow fell closer to the mountains. Of all the reporting stations, Georgetown was the winner with an unbelievable eighty-six inches of snow—with sixty-three inches falling in one day! The city of Denver received forty-six inches, a record that still stands for the single heaviest snowstorm for the city.

Meryl Alberta Eaves Stewart was a child living in Denver when the 1913 storm hit, and years later she recalled it vividly: "The streetcars couldn't run and a big trench was dug down the street so people could get to their houses. It was so deep that all we could see were people's heads above the snowbanks as they walked down the street on their way to work. Men were so exhausted that folks brought them into their homes, set them down in front of big potbelly stoves, and gave them coffee." Ironically, little snow fell over eastern Colorado for the next two months.

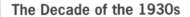

The Decade of the 1930s

In the past one hundred years, the decade between 1930 and 1940 brought some of the wildest weather on record—including heat, drought, dust storms, hail, tornadoes, floods, and extreme cold. The hottest, driest year in Colorado's recorded history was 1934. January 1937 was the coldest month in Colorado history. And from 1934 to 1939, dust-bowl conditions raged over the eastern plains.

A number of conditions combined to create the devastating dust bowls of the late 1930s. As Nolan Doesken explains, "Drought punctuated by dry springs, extremely warm summer temperatures, and strong winds are the necessary ingredients for a dust bowl." Colorado had all three. Also during this time Colorado experienced unusually big floods, enhanced, Doesken notes, "by a lack of vegetation because people had allowed land to become seriously overgrazed, and they farmed land that should not have been cultivated." The impact of this severe weather was amplified by the fact that grasslands were plowed and overgrazed.

The Big Winter Storm of December 29–31, 1951

This storm may possibly be the greatest mountain snowstorm in the history of Colorado. Snowfalls between six and eight feet were common throughout the Colorado high country, accompanied by strong winds. In just three days, thirty-six inches of snow fell in Dillon—almost a quarter of their seasonal average. (And Dillon is a relatively dry place compared to the surrounding mountains.) It's estimated that nearly twice as much snow fell in the higher terrain nearby. "All the mountain roads were closed, mountain communities were cut off for days, and there were countless avalanches," Doesken relates.

The 1965 Summer of Floods

Several days of extremely heavy thunderstorms across much of eastern Colorado resulted in awesome and widespread flooding June 14–18, 1965. The Bijou Creek, near Wiggins, is quoted in *Colorado Centennial 1898–1991* as being "as big as the Mississippi." Several dams failed, including one near Cripple Creek, and damage was extensive. "Denver was hard hit," Doesken notes. "Bridges on I-25 were washed out. It flooded all the way into downtown Denver near Union Station." Many different areas of the state were affected, and the town of Holly recorded 11.08 inches on June 17. "There was even a flash flood on the Blue River in Breckenridge," Doesken adds, "and it is highly unusual to have flash floods that high up."

The marina at Lake Dillon.

The No-Snow Winter of 1976–77

Most severe weather events revolve around a major storm. In the winter of 1976–77, however, it was just the opposite. A persistent high-pressure system over Utah blocked any stormy weather from moving into Colorado for most of the winter season. This system of high pressure helped to push the jet stream well to the north of the state, taking away the prospect of strong winds bringing much moisture to the mountains.

The resulting snow drought was a financial disaster for ski resorts, as nearly all the Colorado ski areas had marginal conditions for almost the entire season. Snow had to be trucked from the Continental Divide to the ski areas in order to create adequate cover at the bases of the mountains. As a result, most Colorado resorts began to add snowmaking capabilities, a technology formerly used only by resorts in the "snow-challenged" midwest and eastern states.

This pattern remained unchanged until March, when finally a huge blizzard developed on the eastern plains. "After months of dry weather," Doesken recalls, "suddenly a big blizzard developed over northeast Colorado. Twenty-foot drifts were commonplace, while the ground was blown clear in other spots." Nine people were killed in the storm.

Air Force bombers dropped bales of hay to starving cattle on the eastern plains.

The Eastern Plains Blizzard of November 2–6, 1946

A massive early season snowstorm enveloped the eastern plains of Colorado during the first week of November 1946, resulting in the deaths of at least thirteen people. This storm began as cold rain on the eastern plains and then quickly turned to snow as a push of chilling air swept down from Canada. The low-pressure center of the storm stalled on the eastern plains and produced persistent snow that finally tallied to several feet. Strong northerly winds whipped the snow into huge drifts that stalled travel by air, road, and rail. Thousands of cattle were stranded and the Air Force dropped bales of hay to try to prevent them from starving.

The Big Thompson Flood of July 31, 1976

One of the greatest weather tragedies in Colorado history, the Big Thompson Flood hit with quick and deadly force. The weekend of July 31–August 1, 1976, was Centennial Weekend in Colorado, marking the one-hundredth anniversary of the state. Thousands of campers and hikers flocked to the high country for a weekend of fun and celebration. By Sunday morning, August 1, the newspapers were filled not with details of the big party but instead with the terrible tragedy in Big Thompson Canyon. A massive thunderstorm developed on the afternoon of July 31, just to the east of Estes Park. This storm grew from routine to dangerous thanks to a combination of light winds aloft and very moist and strong easterly winds at the surface. The easterly surface winds acted as a moisture conveyor system to push humid air well up into the heart of the thunderstorm. The light winds aloft

provided no means to move the storm, so it sat over the same area for several hours. The result: a torrent of rain over a very small, rugged canyon filled with hundreds of unwary picnickers and campers.

The heaviest rainfall, which fell near Glen Haven and Glen Comfort, amounted to nearly twelve inches of rain—seven to eight inches of that falling in just two hours on the evening of the thirty-first. The resulting wall of water was unprecedented. The average stream flow on the Big Thompson River prior to the onset of the rain was only 137 cubic feet per second (cfs). At the peak of the flood at 9:00 P.M., stream flow on the Big Thompson was an unbelievable 31,200 cfs. The first sign of trouble came from Colorado State Patrolman Bob Miller, on duty at Estes Park. Patrolman Miller was asked to drive up and check on reported rock and mud slides on Highway 34 in Big Thompson Canyon. At about 8:35 P.M., Patrolman Miller radioed, "Advise them we have a flood. The whole mountainside is gone. We have people trapped on the other side [of the river]. I'm going to have to move out. I'm up to my doors in water. Advise we can't get to them. I'm going to get out of here before I drown."

Sergeant Hugh Purdy of the Colorado State Patrol never reached his destination. He was driving from Loveland toward Drake, trying to find the headwaters of the flood; his last radio transmission was at approximately 9:15 P.M.: "I'm right in the middle of it. I can't get out . . . about one-half mile east of Drake on the highway. [Tell the cars] to get out of the low area down below." Sergeant Purdy's body was found about eight miles downstream from the site of his last radio transmission. His car was demolished beyond recognition and was identified only by a key ring inscribed with "Colorado State Patrol."

At the mouth of the canyon, a battering ram of water and debris, including big propane tanks, came smashing out onto the plains. The tanks emitted an eerie whistle as they lost pressure. A

THE BIG THOMPSON FLOOD

▥ Weak upper-level winds allowed the storm to remain stationary over the steep, narrow cliffs of Big Thompson Canyon.

▥ The storm gained strength from low-level easterly winds bringing in a steady stream of humid, moist air.

▥ 10 to 12 inches of rain poured into the canyon, with 8 inches falling in less than 2 hours. The steep, rocky canyon walls channeled the rainwater, and the river quickly overflowed its banks and became a flash flood.

WARM, MOIST AIR

huge water siphon—part of a Bureau of Reclamation project—was broken and dislodged by the extreme force. Weighing over 220,000 pounds, this giant pipe was full of another 873,000 pounds of water, bringing the total mass to over a million pounds. The siphon, deeply embedded in the mountainside, "came out like a big soda straw," according to Larimer County Sheriff Bob Watson.

Cleanup efforts lasted for many months, and it took nearly a year to rebuild Highway 34. One hundred thirty-nine people died in the flooding; several bodies were never recovered. The property damage was estimated at $35 million.

The Lessons of the Big Thompson Flood

The Big Thompson Flood of July 31, 1976, was the tragic result of deadly weather in the worst possible location—an unusually fast-moving storm front in a canyon with sheer rock walls incapable of absorbing

moisture. With the memory of 139 lives lost and over $30 million in property damage, Coloradans wonder: Could it happen again?

Perhaps the main outcome of the deadly flood is that it increased awareness of flash floods in the state. One year after Big Thompson Canyon flooded, signs were posted at the entrances of all Front Range canyons with instructions for visitors on the actions they need to take in case of a flash flood. In 1976, many of those killed in the flood died trapped in their cars; decades later, Coloradans know to leave cars behind and climb to safety in such emergencies.

Another difference in Colorado since the 1970s is how we get our weather information. In 1976, the National Weather Service was the only agency involved in meteorology.

Since then, the weather prediction industry has expanded considerably with more meteorologists entering the private sector to work for corporations and the media. The Weather Channel and weather-related web sites also offer more accurate and up-to-date information more quickly than ever before.

Another improvement has been in weather detection and warning systems. Automated stream- and rain-gauge networks are accessed readily by fire departments and emergency management offices, thereby ensuring faster responses to unexpected and potentially dangerous weather changes.

If you are heading into areas of high risk for flash floods, be sure to stay in contact with a source of weather information and heed all posted warning signs. If you do encounter a flash flood, climb to the highest point in the area and never try to drive through floodwaters. Flash floods usually subside quickly; sometimes all it takes to survive is a little patience.

The "Seven-Eleven Hailstorm" of 1990

The second most costly hailstorm in U.S. history, this storm stretched from north of Fort Collins almost all the way to Colorado Springs. Midafternoon on July 11, the storm began by feeding on a combination of moist easterly surface winds and a cool pool of air aloft. The chilly air in the higher reaches of the atmosphere allowed for the formation of large hailstones.

Nolan Doesken notes, "This long-lived hailstorm traveled from Estes Park to Colorado Springs in three hours and went directly over Denver." The storm was a huge media event as local Denver television and radio stations and newspapers provided extensive, immediate coverage. The hail hit so quickly that surprised and panicked people trapped on amusement rides at Elitch Gardens were cut and bruised by the large hail.

More than $600,000,000 in property losses were reported. "Roofers had incredible business," Doesken recalls. Next to the tens of thousands of damaged roofs, automobiles were the next casualty. Windshields were smashed by hail that ranged in size from marbles to tennis balls. The hoods and trunks of cars and trucks retained an eerie likeness to the surface of the moon for many months after the storm as body shops struggled to catch up. Its catchy name based on the date, the "Seven-Eleven" storm made an indelible impression on Coloradans and their pocketbooks.

The July 1997 Flood

The first half of the summer of 1997 was very hot and dry over eastern Colorado. As concern mounted over drought conditions and fire danger through the first two weeks of July, a massive El Niño event was building in the central Pacific Ocean. This warm-water

anomaly usually manifests itself in the form of unusual winter weather. In 1997, however, El Niño was so strong it began to affect summertime weather patterns as well. By late July every year, Colorado begins to come under the influence of a moist southerly wind pattern that brings humid air into the state. This is the so-called monsoon flow that creates most of the mid-to-late summer thunderstorm activity in the state. The immense heat and moisture from El Niño added fuel to the fire of the average summer monsoon in

Colorado. From late July through mid-August, rain fell on almost a daily basis. Many areas received over eight inches of rain in just three to four weeks—about half the average annual total for most places in eastern Colorado.

On the night of July 28, a small but nearly stationary thunderstorm began to dump heavy rains on the southwest side of Fort Collins. This storm did not look like anything special on radar, but very light winds aloft allowed it to stay parked over the same area for several hours. Doesken recalls that this storm delivered the heaviest rain over an urban area ever recorded in Colorado. At its most intense point, "fourteen inches of rain were recorded in one day." The heavy rain fell over a narrow drainage basin that passed under a railroad bridge. Unfortunately, the railroad bed acted as a dam for the rising water, which could not flow quickly enough through the opening under the bridge. When a plugged culvert under the railroad bed finally gave way to the tremendous pressure of the water, a giant wall of water swept into a nearby mobile home park. The result was both eerie and tragic. Floodwaters mixed with flames as the trailers were detached from their foundations and gas lines ruptured and caught fire. Rescuers struggled amidst the flames to try to get people out of their homes. Despite their valiant efforts, five people died in the flood. In addition, millions of dollars in damage was reported on the Colorado State University campus as a result of the flooding. Thousands of valuable books were lost when the floodwaters poured into the basement of one of the campus libraries.

The following night, as eastern Colorado was still reeling from the events of the past twenty-four hours, another massive flood hit the northeast plains. Pawnee Creek near Sterling flooded a large area of Logan County, destroying crops and damaging homes. "This was an even bigger storm than the one that flooded Fort Collins the day before," Doesken notes. "At least thirteen inches of rain fell at the storm's center on the evening of July 29, 1997, just northeast of Fort Collins near Stoneham."

The Christmas Blizzard of 1982.

A lightning-sparked fire, 1956.

Other Major Weather Events

There are many other major weather events that have made big news around Colorado in the past century. Some of those storms might seem to be the "greatest of all time" to those who are unlucky enough to experience them. However, many storms —albeit severe— turn out to be very localized. A good case in point is the Christmas Blizzard of 1982—a tremendous storm, but one that really zeroed in on the Denver area. The Limon Tornado in 1990 is another good example of a noteworthy storm that affected a relatively small area.

There have been many terrible cold waves in the wintertime. In 1983, the days before Christmas felt like Santa Claus had sent the North Pole down as an envoy. Temperatures fell below zero for nearly eighty straight hours in the Denver area. A severe cold wave in 1951 gripped the state in record chill. On the first of February, the temperature bottomed out at sixty below zero at Taylor Park Dam and hit forty below along the Front Range, killing many cherry orchards. Denver dropped to –25 degrees and Fort Collins hit –40 degrees. "This storm changed the landscape of the Front Range," Doesken says. "It killed fruit orchards and scared fruit growers away for many years. Fruit growers are now finally reestablishing themselves."

Massive and devastating storms, however, are punctuation marks to an overall Colorado climate that is quite enjoyable. The "three hundred days of sunshine" may still be the hook that brings people to our state, but newcomers soon learn that Colorado weather is a lot like the girl with the tiny curl, right in the middle of her forehead: When it is good, it is very, very good—but when it is bad, it is horrid!

Denver snowstorm of 1913.

Top Nine Winter Facts

1. The coldest New Year's Day: 1979, when a morning temperature of -60 degrees F was reported in Maybell.

2. Worst winter snowstorm: December 1–5, 1913, when 46 inches of the white stuff fell in Denver, and a whopping 86 inches fell in Georgetown.

3. Most damaging windstorm: From 1 A.M. to 9 A.M. on January 17, 1982, when a potent down slope windstorm clobbered the Front Range. Winds blew up to 120 miles per hour on Table Mesa in Boulder. Statewide damage exceeded $17 million.

4. The infamous Christmas Blizzard of 1982 buried Denver under 3 feet of snow and brought to a halt all travel into and out of the city for 48 hours.

5. January's highest recorded temperature: 84 degrees F, recorded in Hoehne near Trinidad in 1910.

6. Highest barometric pressure ever measured in Colorado: 31.32 inches, reported on December 14, 1964, in Alamosa.

7. The "Alaska Blaster" of February 1–7, 1989, postponed some of the World Cup ski races at Vail when the cold front swooped south, ushering in subzero temperatures and heavy snow.

8. Strangest winter "fog storm": For ten days in February, 1978, fog covered the eastern plains. Miles of power lines snapped under the weight of accumulated rime ice.

9. Did you know? Nighttime temperatures in winter are typically colder in the valleys than in the surrounding mountains.

Top Nine Spring Facts

1. Most powerful thunder snowstorm: March 8, 1990. More than 18 inches of heavy, wet snow fell on the Front Range in under 6 hours. Motorists trapped in the blizzard reported that their windshield wipers were snapped off by heavy snow and high winds.

2. Twenty-four inches of rain in 24 hours reportedly fell near Kiowa during a storm in May 1935.

3. A remarkably strong cold front visibly crossed Colorado on April 7, 1987, when **temperatures plunged over 50 degrees** in one afternoon and 3 inches of snow fell on Denver in the evening.

4. Severe flooding occurred along the Front Range May 4–7, 1969, when 9.02 inches of rain fell in Evergreen over four days.

5. Denver's heaviest official rainfall: 6.53 inches, which fell in 24 hours May 21–22, 1976.

6. On May 27, 1898, in Denver, **0.97 inches of rain fell in 10 minutes.**

7. The deepest high-country snow depths of the season are reported in April, when they average between 60 and 100 inches. Wolf Creek Pass accumulated 838 inches of snow after the winter of 1978–1979— that's over 69 feet of snow!

8. May 2 is the average date of the **last spring freeze** in Denver.

9. Did you know? March is typically the snowiest month in Colorado. Intense spring storms can drop as much as 5 inches of snow an hour.

Denver, 1969.

Top Nine Summer Facts

1. Hottest summer temperature statewide: 114 degrees F, recorded on two different days—first on July 1, 1933, in Las Animas, and also on July 11, 1954, in Sedgwick.

2. Denver's hottest day: August 8, 1978, when the mercury hit 105 degrees F.

3. Snowiest Independence Day: 1993, when snowstorms canceled fireworks and frustrated campers in Colorado's mountains.

4. Hail 3 inches in diameter fell continuously for 45 minutes on June 13, 1984, in Arvada, causing over $200 million in damage.

5. Colorado's deadliest tornado hit the town of Thurman on August 10, 1924, with 10 fatalities.

6. An extremely early freeze happened in Colorado over the night August 25–26, 1910.

7. June is Colorado's severe weather month, with an average of 15 tornadoes and 46 damaging hailstorms every year.

8. Summertime temperatures decrease systematically with elevation in Colorado, losing 5 to 6 degrees F with every 1,000 feet.

9. Did you know? Nearly all Colorado hail falls between 1 P.M. and 9 P.M.

Top Nine Autumn Facts

1. Deadliest autumn snowstorm on the Front Range: November 2–6, 1946, with 20–50 inches of snow falling over most of the plains. Thirteen people died.

2. Earliest costly snowstorm: September 16–18, 1971, when 1 to 2 feet of snow fell from Fort Collins to Pueblo. The damage caused by broken tree branches totaled in the millions.

3. After a mild autumn, a **severe early cold wave** killed thousands of trees and shrubs over eastern Colorado from October 27 to November 2, 1991. On October 30, 1991, the high temperature was only 21 degrees F.

4. The **heaviest rains** in southwestern Colorado occur in October; 12.42 inches of rain fell at Vallecito Dam in October 1972.

5. The Silverton-Durango train service was interrupted for 60 days in October 1911, when heavy rains caused flooding in the San Juan Mountains.

6. September is the **least cloudy month** in Colorado.

7. October 7 is the average date for the **first autumn freeze** in Denver.

8. First official weather observation in Denver: November 20, 1871, taken by Henry Fenton.

9. Did you know? Although it is commonly stated that Colorado enjoys 300 days of sunshine a year, there has never been any data to support the idea. The first time this was mentioned was in an 1870 newspaper article.

Pueblo, 1921.

Storm CHASING

"Toto, I have a feeling we're not in Kansas anymore."

—Dorothy, *Wizard of Oz*

There is a certain romance and danger about driving into some of the most severe storms on the planet. Each spring, hundreds of storm chasers, both amateur and professional, seek out the heart of a severe thunderstorm in the hopes of catching a glimpse of the holy grail of weather—the tornado. Some of these storm chasers may have gotten their first thirst to see a twister as children when they saw the *Wizard of Oz.* That Hollywood tornado (with special effects thanks to a rayon stocking), still looks ominous and pretty realistic even after sixty years. The newest generation of storm chasers may look back at the movie *Twister* as the catalyst for their initial thrust into the art. Whatever the reason, storm chasers go after tornadoes with a frenzy that can rival a prospector searching for gold.

Like those early prospectors, most tornado chasers come up empty-handed many more times than they strike pay dirt. And unlike the *Wizard of Oz,* where the tornado came to Dorothy, or *Twister,* where the chasers witnessed over a half dozen tornadoes in one twenty-four-hour period, actual tornadoes are pretty hard to come by. There are about one hundred thousand thunderstorms every year in the United States. Of those, about ten thousand are classified as "severe"—winds of at least fifty-eight miles per hour, hail three-quarters of an inch or larger, and/or very heavy rainfall. Of the ten thousand severe storms, only about one thousand tornadoes are produced each year. So in essence, one percent of all thunderstorms actually produce a tornado. The average life span of a tornado is about ten minutes, and the average path length is only a mile or two. Tornado chasing really is the meteorological equivalent of searching for a needle in a haystack.

Most experienced tornado chasers will tell you that the biggest risk from driving all over the countryside is not getting hit by the tornado, but rather getting a "square butt" from sitting in the car so long! There are other risks involved in this endeavor: car

Kathy Sabine: Mild-Mannered Weathercaster or Super Storm Chaser?

"It's amazing to see what Mother Nature can do with one little cloud," says Kathy Sabine, and she should know. In addition to her duties forecasting KUSA-TV in Denver, Kathy Sabine is an avid storm chaser. She has turned her love for pursuing dramatic weather into a Heartland Regional Emmy for her on-scene report of two tornadoes that touched down simultaneously on May 30, 1996.

That day began, Sabine recalls, like any other day. "My on-air duties included filling in for the morning weathercaster who was on vacation, so I started my day at 2 A.M.," she remembers. By noon, an area of low pressure set up, producing counterclockwise winds that can turn an ordinary cumulus cloud into a tornado producer. Low-level moisture increased, and dew points were in the low fifties. "When the satellite indicated a weather disturbance heading in that afternoon," Sabine says, "I knew something was going to happen. I just hoped we could get to the right place at the right time."

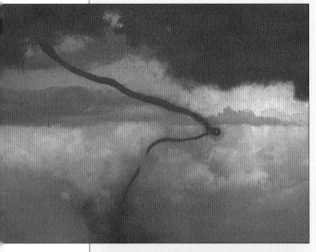

By 1:30 P.M., the National Weather Service issued a Tornado Watch. Sabine and photojournalist Eric Kehe headed northeast on I-76 toward a convergence line, where, Sabine explains, "winds cause a horizontal net inflow of air over a specified area."

"At 4:00 P.M., we heard from the producer that the station wanted a live shot to show the developing weather," she continues. "After Eric set up the camera, the sky got darker, the winds picked up—and was it? Maybe—yes! It was a tiny needle of a funnel cloud forming just behind us! Unbelievable! What timing!"

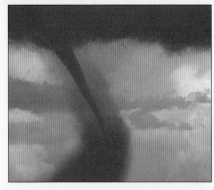

That first funnel went right back up into the clouds, but as Sabine and Kehe drove a little closer, near the town of Wiggins, another funnel appeared. "Suddenly I saw swirling dirt at the surface! It had touched down in an open field," Sabine relates.

At 4:40 P.M., "we had a fully formed tornado on the ground, clear as day," Sabine says. "We threw the gear in the back of the news car and drove closer to an overpass near a gas station where bystanders looked on in awe. Eric pulled people into camera view, and with the tornado visible over their shoulders, he asked them to comment on what they saw and how they were feeling."

As the interviews progressed, Sabine reported what she was seeing—but what she was seeing was not one but two tornadoes, side by side. "Two tornadoes on the ground at the same time from the same wall cloud—this was a once-in-a-lifetime experience, and Eric and I had it on tape!" she recalls. "The second tornado became very snakelike at times, jutting from side to side and coiling around itself. It was an ominous and eerie sight, appearing as if it had a life of its own . . . and this was when I started to feel a little fear instead of the adrenaline rush."

Through her live reports, Sabine was able to give residents exact coordinates and information on storm movement. After the tornadoes dissipated, the story shifted to the storm's damage and survivors. Sabine arrived back at the station around 12:30 A.M. the next day—a 22-hour day!

As a child, Sabine dreamed of becoming a veterinarian. Her bachelor's degree in journalism from Cal Poly State University earned her a position as a weather forecaster in San Luis Obispo, where her mentor was woman meteorologist Sharon Graves. Sabine's advice to girls interested in meteorology? Focus on math, science, and language skills, study hard, and watch the skies!

trouble, falling asleep at the wheel, hydroplaning in heavy rain, hail damage, and being struck by lightning. Still sound like fun? Well, if you are still interested, here are some guidelines to storm chasing.

There are *three basic things* that are very important to successful storm chasing. First, be sure that you have a *dependable vehicle.* In Colorado and western Kansas, there is a tremendous amount of open space and certainly no service station or towing company around the corner. It is vitally important to be prepared in case of a breakdown. Check over all aspects of your car's health, but also be ready to handle minor road repairs—possibly in the dark or the rain.

Second, have an excellent set of *maps*—the more detailed the better. Go to a good map store and buy the latest book of state and county roads available. You'll need to know all the little side roads and the condition of those roads—tornadoes don't always follow the interstate!

Gas up the car, pack a good lunch, and keep your fingers crossed!

Finally, the most important thing to know about storm chasing is *meteorology*—you must be savvy about the general weather pattern in order to determine when and where a severe storm will erupt. Even more important, you need to understand storm structure in order to know where the tornado will form from the severe thunderstorm. This last point is critical because it might save your life! Obviously we are talking about a dangerous hobby—you are literally driving into the "belly of the beast."

A supercell

As I noted in earlier chapters, most tornadoes develop from massive churning thunderstorms called "supercells." These rotating thunderstorms form with a

combination of strong temperature and humidity gradients and increasing wind shear as you go higher in the atmosphere. The low-level temperature and humidity changes help to spark the initial thunderstorm, and the vertical wind shear helps to create a long-lasting rotating thunderstorm. The best time for these types of storms to blossom is in the spring and early summer. At that time of year, there is still a large temperature contrast from north to south across the nation. As the increasing warmth of the air over the Gulf of Mexico pushes northward, it clashes with the leftover chill of winter. The result of this meeting of the air masses is seldom quiet, and big thunderstorms are the by-product. In addition, the jet-stream winds tend to be quite strong in the spring and early summer, so those powerful winds aloft bring in the vertical wind shear that gets everything spinning. The prime time for storm chasing in the United States begins in mid-March and lasts until about the Fourth of July. Storm-chasing season first starts in Texas in March and then slowly works its way to the north and west. Oklahoma and Kansas enter into the picture in April and early May. By the middle of May, Colorado is shaking off its winter coat

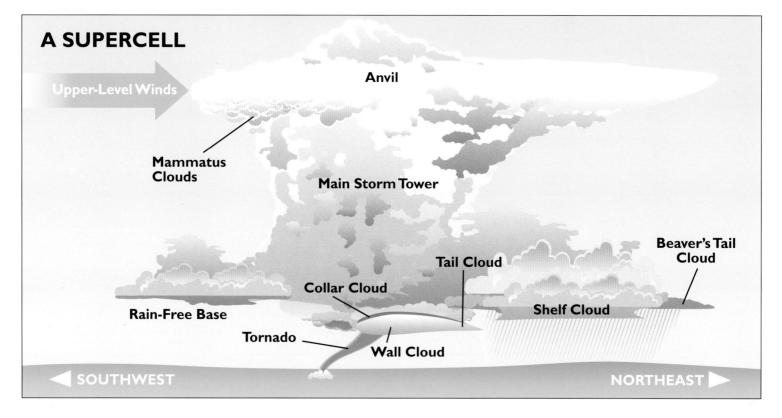

A SUPERCELL

Upper-Level Winds

Anvil

Mammatus Clouds

Main Storm Tower

Beaver's Tail Cloud

Tail Cloud

Collar Cloud

Shelf Cloud

Rain-Free Base

Tornado

Wall Cloud

◄ SOUTHWEST

NORTHEAST ►

and getting set to enter the severe thunderstorm season. Although we get tornado-producing storms in May, the most active season for Colorado is early June.

By the first two weeks of June, the atmosphere has warmed sufficiently to fire off severe thunderstorms, hail, and tornadoes on just about any day over eastern Colorado. If you throw in a weather front or a strong current of jet-stream winds, the odds increase dramatically. Television forecasts on 9NEWS or the Weather Channel can provide you with a good idea of when a particularly stormy day may be on the way. This will allow you to plan a storm-chasing trip a day or so ahead of time. Remember my point at the start of this chapter—storm chasing is dangerous! In addition, the odds are in your favor that you will spend a lot of time driving around and very little time, if any, actually witnessing a tornado.

If you are serious about this endeavor, I strongly suggest that you first take the time to read as much as possible about severe storms and tornadoes and that you attend a "SkyWarn" meeting. The SkyWarn program is set up to train spotters on what to look for and how to stay out of danger during severe weather events. SkyWarn spotters are most frequently ham radio enthusiasts who use their radio skills to relay valuable information to the National Weather Service. The truth is, most ham operators would probably prefer not to see a bunch of video-camera-equipped storm-chaser "wannabees" out on the roads, as it greatly increases the risk of a collision. Nevertheless, if you are properly trained in storm-chase protocol and know where to look, you can be of some value. For more information about SkyWarn meetings, call your local National Weather Service office.

In Search of the Supercell

Here are some basic tips about where to look and what to look for. (Let me emphasize again how important it is to go to a SkyWarn training session before you head out to track a twister!) Most tornadoes form on the southwest side of a supercell thunder-

FUNNEL FORMATION

Below the storm, a rolling column of air is created from updrafts of warm, moist air and plummeting downdrafts of cool air.

Shifting downdrafts push down on the rolling column and begin to tilt it vertically.

Warm updrafts also influence the tilting and stretch the whirling winds upwards toward the storm.

The spinning column of air connects with the storm's mesocyclone and becomes a tornado. The vortex at the base of the funnel sucks up dirt and debris, making the tornado visible.

storm. This is due to the complex rotating structure of the supercell. The moist low-level inflow that feeds the storm comes in from the south or southeast, ahead of the main body of the storm. This air rises up into the heart of the severe storm and helps to form the main tower of the thunderstorm. The increasing winds aloft create wind shears that begin to turn the tower toward the northeast in a slow rotation. As the tower grows into the stable air of the stratosphere, the lifting stops and the top of the thunderstorm is blown off into the familiar "anvil" shape. When the anvil forms, you have a mature thunderstorm that can produce rain, wind, and hail. The heaviest precipitation tends to fall on the northeast side of the storm, ahead of the strongest updraft. Think of the updraft as a conveyor belt that carries low-level moisture up into the center of the storm and then pushes that moisture out to the east or northeast by way of the stronger upper-level winds. As the rain and hail fall back down, the air is cooled and it sinks toward earth. At this point, complicated circulations develop that create a swirling downdraft toward the southwest edge of the storm. This sinking, rotating air is what helps to create the tornado.

If it has occurred to you that approaching the thunderstorm from the south or southeast side makes sense, you may be on the right track as a storm chaser. If the storm is moving from west to east or southwest toward the northeast as most of them do, then a south or southeast approach will allow you to spot the tornado from a position of good visibility. By following the southern edge of the storm, you will not be in the bands of heavy rain and hail and should be in a better location to actually see the tornado. The greatest danger in storm chasing is getting hit by a tornado that is wrapped in rain. This is most likely to happen if you try to "punch the core" of the storm by driving into the storm cell from the north or northeast.

Appraching a storm from the south or southeast is the safest.

Thunderstorms are all unique—you may not find the textbook case, but most often the best and safest odds are from a southern approach. You still may face rain, large hail, and the ever-present risk of being hit by lightning, but chances are you'll see more tornadoes and live to tell about it by using that south or southeast rule of thumb.

A good set of road maps is a valuable asset in storm chasing. You need to be able to plan your trip so as to allow yourself an escape route in the event that things get too intense. By keeping an eye on the storm and knowing that you have an alternate route, you should be able to get out of the way if necessary. Remember, thunderstorms can do strange things and you can quickly find yourself in a dangerous spot. Keep a watchful eye on the sky all around you—including directly overhead! Never wait too long to abandon a spotting site if the weather is closing in fast. Also, avoid the temptation to get too close to the storm. The most destructive

Keep a close eye on the sky all around you —including directly overhead!

Tim Samaras: A Day in the Life of a Storm Chaser

Storm chasers are a breed apart in meteorology circles, keeping track of climate changes on home computers and equipping their vehicles with weather-monitoring instruments. When dramatic weather hits Colorado, storm chasers hit the road in dogged pursuit.

Storm chaser Tim Samaras, who frequently assists local weather stations, described the chase that occurred on October 5, 1994, as particularly successful. Samaras drives a specially equipped van and is well known locally for his dramatic weather photography.

"The atmosphere was primed for severe weather" when Samaras awoke at 4:30 A.M. and discovered on the internet that Limon, Burlington, Lamar, and Akron on the eastern plains were registering high dew points and winds of up to 35 miles per hour. Having arranged with his boss to take half the day off, Samaras left work at 11:30 A.M. and headed for a target area between Limon and Punkin Center. As he drove, the eastern horizon looked deceptively calm with small cumulus clouds hugging the foothills behind him.

At 2:30 P.M., Samaras pulled off the road outside of the town of Genoa to get a reading on his psychrometer, which measures the moisture in the air. The instrument indicated a higher than usual dew point—and the possibility of a huge storm. Having found the right place, Samaras then had to wait for the right time. He says, "A very valuable lesson that I learned over my years of storm chasing is that it is better to be early for a storm than late!"

A few hours' wait was worth the effort. Watching thunderheads build slowly to the southwest about 45 miles away, Samaras knew that his patience had paid off when he heard a National Weather Service tornado watch announced for most of eastern Colorado.

Samaras jumped in his vehicle and headed south on Highway 71 to set up his video camera just outside of Punkin Center. Surface winds increased to 40 miles per hour from the southeast, and the cumulus clouds raced across the sky. The thunderstorm turned westward toward Samaras and began to display "a very pronounced rotating wall cloud, a precursor to the beginnings of a tornado."

Dodging lightning strikes, Samaras drove 15 miles north on Highway 71, pulled into a cornfield, and videotaped a small funnel cloud that reached for the ground but finally lifted back into the clouds. In full chase mode, he drove back to Limon and then north on I-70 "to keep pace with the beast."

At 5:30 P.M., as he crested a hilltop near Cedar Point, Samaras met the beast eye to eye when a large funnel cloud dropped out of the thunderstorm base. It touched the ground and churned up the open fields with dirt and debris filling its rotating columns. Samaras reported the tornado to the National Weather Service via the local SkyWarn net, using the ham radio equipment in his van. He then turned his camera to face the storm:

"The tornado assumed an elephant-trunk-like shape as the storm continued to move to the north. The touchdown point did not move. As the tornado weakened, something remarkable happened that I have never seen. The upper two thirds of the tornado just disappeared, leaving the bottom part on the ground. The vortex on the ground continued to churn away for another minute, and then at 6:03 P.M. it simply vanished."

The rotating wall cloud persisted as it crossed I-70, but produced no more tornadoes that day. As Samaras drove home, cool air moved into the area and the radio forecasted light snow for the foothills that night. Only in Colorado!

winds are very close to the tornado, but debris can fly far from the funnel and be a major hazard (remember the flying cows in *Twister*!).

Tornado Clues

There are some cloud formations that are common with tornado-producing storms. The one that is most often mentioned is the *wall cloud.* The wall cloud is a lowering of the cloud base near the region of intense thunderstorm updraft and is formed when the strong updraft draws rain-cooled air from the front of the thunderstorm upward. This upward motion creates a lowered cloud base as the moisture in the air condenses. The wall cloud will usually have a slow but steady counterclockwise rotation and may not be associated with heavy rain or hail. Often, the heavy precipitation is just to the northeast and the wall cloud is visible in what is called the "rain-free" area. Only about half of the wall clouds observed actually spawn a tornado, so if you see one, watch it for several minutes to see what happens next. A dangerous wall cloud that is about to produce a tornado will have a strong rotation. From this rotating base, the tornado will begin to grow down toward the ground. At this point you may in fact already have a tornado on the ground, even if you cannot see it.

Wall cloud

If you see a wall cloud, watch it for several minutes to see what happens next.

Remember that tornadoes are just rotating columns of air—and air is invisible. The classic tornadoes seen on television and in movies are made visible by clouds and debris. Look at the ground under the wall cloud and the developing funnel, and check for any signs of swirling dust. It may be that the rotation of the air has already reached the ground even if the condensation funnel has not. This is particularly important in eastern Colorado, where the air is relatively dry. Often our tornadoes show rotation at the base of the cloud, then nothing in between until you see the swirl of dust on the ground. Even

without the classic tornado shape, it is still a tornado capable of doing damage.

A *collar cloud* is an accessory cloud that surrounds the wall cloud. You could call this the "turtle neck collar" of clouds. It rotates at a slower rate than the wall cloud, but is worth noting. Another type of cloud often seen with a supercell thunderstorm is what is called the *Beaver's Tail.* This cloud enters the northeast side of the updraft portion of the storm and has the appearance of the tail of a beaver. The Beaver's Tail is an indication of strong low-level moisture inflow into the storm. The Beaver's Tail is a good sign that the storm has the strong wind shears needed to foster a tornado.

Sometimes confused with the Beaver's Tail is another cloud simply called the *Tail Cloud.* The Tail Cloud is much smaller in scope than the Beaver's Tail and looks like a thin tail or needle-shaped cloud near the wall cloud. It usually forms on the north side of the wall cloud and looks like a tail pointing toward the area of heaviest precipitation (usually toward the north-east). A Tail Cloud forms at a lower level than a Beaver's Tail and is farther back toward the southwest part of the thunderstorm.

Tail cloud

Striations or stripes that form on the sides of a thunderstorm are good signs of rotation. These rings that form on the clouds are an excellent indication that the storm is a strong supercell that may

Shelf cloud

produce a tornado. Striations occasionally form on wall clouds as well. A *shelf cloud* is a common sight along the leading edge of a severe thunderstorm. This low-level cloud looks like a dark wedge attached to the front of the storm. The shelf cloud is associated with gusty straight-line winds ahead of the storm

and is caused by the condensation of water vapor as warm air rises over the cool low-level outflow from the storm. This type of cloud may show signs of rotating, but it will do so along a horizontal axis. The shelf cloud is sometimes called an *arc cloud* or *arcus cloud*. Shelf clouds are not tornadoes (although they are sometimes mistaken for them), but they are associated with straight-line winds that can cause some damage.

The anvil of a supercell

Similar to the shelf cloud, the *roll cloud* is an ominous sight ahead of an approaching thunderstorm. The roll cloud is a low-level cloud that moves or rolls along ahead of the gusty straight-line winds of a thunderstorm. It differs from a shelf cloud in that it is not attached to the rest of the thunderstorm, but simply rolls out ahead. Although they look scary, roll clouds are actually formed when the downdraft is weakening. The roll cloud breaks away from the parent thunderstorm and slowly dies away as the rest rolls on ahead. Although they can cause strong straight-line winds, roll clouds usually look worse than they really are.

Cumulo-nimbus mammatus clouds sound scary, but in fact they are no threat at all. These are the odd-looking, bubble-shaped clouds you can see on the underside of thunderstorm anvils. They are caused by rain-cooled air that condenses on the outside of the cumulo-nimbus cloud. Mammatus clouds are not dangerous in themselves, nor do they produce a tornado. They are signs of strong turbulence within the parent thunderstorm, however, and are usually seen with storms that are causing severe weather. The mammatus cloud makes for some spectacular pictures as they are often visibly backlit by the setting sun as the storm moves away to the east.

Mammatus clouds

Scud clouds sound rather frightening (especially after the Gulf War), but in weather terminology, they are simply scraps of low clouds that swirl around under a severe storm. They are moist leftovers from all the business up above. These cloud fragments can give a surreal appearance to the sky, but they are just signs of plenty of moisture and turbulence in the air.

Other Types of Tornadoes

The supercell thunderstorm is the most common producer of a tornado, but there are others. A tornado is, of course, just a rapidly rotating column of air, so there can be other mechanisms for creating them. However, there are two other types of tornadoes commonly seen in Colorado that are worth discussing—the *gustnado* and the *landspout.*

The gustnado (or gustinado as it is sometimes called) is a slang term for a gust-front tornado. This type of tornado is small and usually weak and short-lived. Gustnados form on the leading edge or gust front of a thunderstorm and are caused by swirling wind motions in the local area that come together vertically for a brief period of time. A good way to visualize a gustnado is to think of the swirling

A gustnado

eddies that spin off in the water from the bow wake of a boat. These "mini-tornadoes" are sometimes only visible as a debris cloud or a dust whirl near the ground. Because gustnados form on

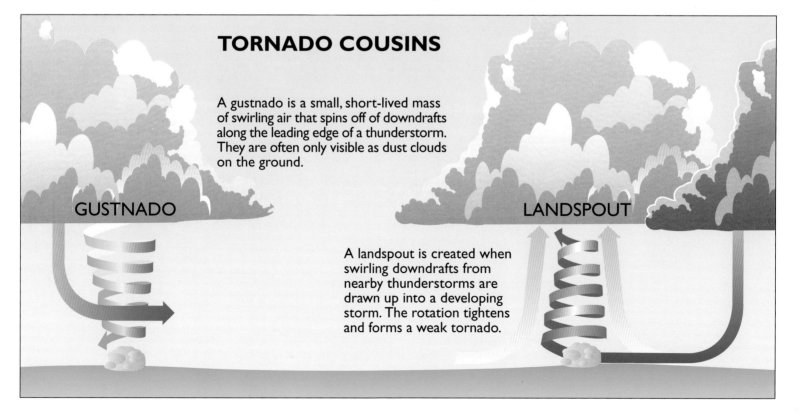

TORNADO COUSINS

A gustnado is a small, short-lived mass of swirling air that spins off of downdrafts along the leading edge of a thunderstorm. They are often only visible as dust clouds on the ground.

GUSTNADO

LANDSPOUT

A landspout is created when swirling downdrafts from nearby thunderstorms are drawn up into a developing storm. The rotation tightens and forms a weak tornado.

the leading edge of the storm, they are not usually associated with classic supercell thunderstorm structure and generally are more likely to be seen in with a shelf cloud instead of with a wall cloud. Recent studies have shown that gustnados can form on the edges of straight-line downburst wind events. The analogy of this would be the swirling patterns that form when you pull a canoe paddle through through the water. These gustnados are sometimes called "bookend tornadoes" because one will form on each end of a strong straight-line wind event. They can cause some confusion in determining whether a storm was a tornado or a downburst as the resulting damage has both straight and spinning characteristics. In fact, this type of storm is a hybrid—both a downburst and a tornado!

Small, intense thunderstorms like this make landspouts common along the Front Range.

The *landspout* is another form of weak tornado that is often seen in Colorado. This type of small twister is formed when colliding wind boundaries from several thunderstorms come together to create a swirling low-level circulation. This whirl of wind is then drawn into the updraft of a developing thunderstorm. As the swirling winds are drawn into the storm, the rotation tightens up, much as figure skaters spin faster as they pull their arms in. These twisters are really closer to dust devils than tornadoes. The landspout tornado is common along the Front Range because the topography of the area tends to concentrate low-level wind circulations and because we get a lot of small but intense thunderstorms that help to create numerous outflow boundaries. Landspouts are not associated with wall clouds or classic tornado structures. Instead, they can form under a rapidly developing thunderstorm that might not even produce rain. Landspouts seldom last long and rarely do any damage, but they are technically tornadoes. Although we usually do issue warnings on television for landspouts and gustnados, we try to mention that these are smaller, less-threatening storms than the classic supercell tornado. Nevertheless, they tend to be much more common in the Denver area than supercell tornadoes, so we do need to keep an eye out for them. Even a landspout can be destructive if it touches down in a neighborhood.

A landspout

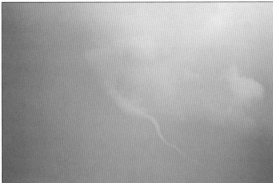

A rare waterspout over Boulder.

Because our state is semi-arid, we generally do not have to worry too much about *waterspouts*. A waterspout is simply a tornado that forms or moves over water. Although chances are slim, waterspouts have happened in Colorado. In the summer of 1997, a tornado developed near the Boulder Reservoir and was even photographed over the water—technically a waterspout, but just barely.

One last type of tornado bears mentioning—the *cold air funnel,* a very distant relative of the classic supercell tornado. Cold air funnels are small, weak twisters that can develop from a small rain shower or thunderstorm when the air aloft is very cold and unstable. The cold air funnel rarely touches the ground and is usually seen as just a thin tail of spinning clouds. These funnels often develop *after* a cold front has pushed through the area and the atmosphere is still somewhat turbulent. Cold air funnels are rarely dangerous, and usually we don't issue a warning for them.

Storm chasers often discuss the success of their mission by comparing the size and strength of the tornadoes they have seen. The most commonly used basis of comparison is the "Fujita Scale" or "F Scale." The Fujita Scale of tornado intensity was developed by Dr. Theodore Fujita of the University of Chicago. Dr. Fujita wanted to create a way of categorizing the 700 to 1,000 tornadoes that strike the United States each year. The scale that he developed is based on wind damage to buildings and trees hit by the tornado. All tornadoes and most other severe local windstorms are assigned a single number from this scale.

The Fujita Scale

F0	40–72 mph	light damage	Weak tornadoes
F1	73–112 mph	moderate damage	Weak tornadoes
F2	113–157 mph	considerable damage	Strong tornadoes
F3	158–206 mph	severe damage	Strong tornadoes
F4	207–260 mph	devastating damage	Violent tornadoes
F5	261–318 mph	incredible damage	Violent tornadoes

The Fujita Scale is very useful in documenting and relaying how strong a tornado is, but it does have one drawback, especially in Colorado. If a very powerful tornado hits nothing but an open field, how do you classify it? Storm chasers I've spoken with are quite sure that Colorado has seen a few F4 and F5 tornadoes way out on the eastern plains. But since there is very little large-scale construction out there, all these storms do is what I call "natural crop rotation." In a similar fashion, a relatively weak landspout could touch down in Aurora and really tear up a neighborhood.

With practice, you can learn to classify a tornado by its overall size and appearance as well as by the structure of the parent thunderstorm—a classic supercell is more likely to produce a strong or violent tornado. In the United States, 80 percent of all tornadoes are classified F0 or F1. About 17 percent reach the F2 to F3 classification, and only 2 to 3 percent become F4 or F5. However, the vast majority of tornado deaths are caused by F2 through F5 tornadoes. If you still have the urge to go find one, please be sure you know what you are looking for and be aware of the risks. Gas up the car, pack a good lunch, and keep your fingers crossed!

Meteorology or MEDIA-ROLOGY?

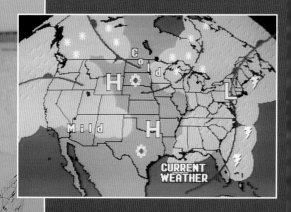

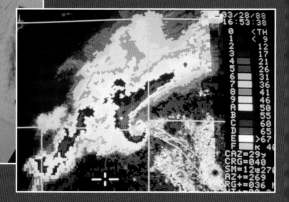

I've always wanted to be a meteorologist. In second grade, I remember reading the *How and Why Wonder Book of Weather* at least a dozen times. Growing up in Madison, Wisconsin, I was fascinated by the weather and often ventured into the front yard during thunderstorms. I didn't mind getting wet—I just wanted a closer look at the lightning. Mom would yell, "Get in the house now, you silly kid!"

Trees were bent in the wind, lightning slashed across the sky, hail pounded the ground, and the street was beginning to flood. In other words, it was really cool!

One storm was particularly memorable. We were in the middle of a heat wave, with 95- to 100-degree highs every day for a week. A cold front was supposed to bring us some nice cool air. On the night the front moved in, I was in my bedroom listening to the radio. Suddenly the song was interrupted by a special weather bulletin: a tornado watch had been issued for the area. Big storms were developing to the west, with the potential to produce large hail, dangerous lightning, very heavy rains, and possibly tornadoes! When I heard this, I did what any intelligent person would do—I ran to the window, threw it open, and waited for the storm to hit! Way off in the distance, I could see a murky cloud gradually getting bigger and darker and closer. I got closer as well —so close that my nose was pushed against the window screen. The air was very still, and then I began to hear a roaring sound. The roar grew louder and louder—and suddenly the storm hit. Wind ripped through the open window, and I was literally blown back into the middle of my room. I struggled back to the window and could hardly believe my eyes. Trees were bent in the wind and lightning slashed across the sky, hail pounded the ground, and the street was beginning to flood. In other words, it was really cool!

Then the tornado sirens went off. "Great!" I said. "I get to see a tornado, too!" But then I felt something on the collar of my shirt—my mother's hand, pulling me down to the basement where it was safe. As soon as we got down the steps and she let me go,

I raced back up to get another look. But she was right behind me, ready to haul me back down again!

I had to miss the rest of the storm. (As I mentioned earlier, it's very important to find a safe place during a heavy storm or tornado—a lesson I learned quickly!) But my love of weather was born.

My Homemade Weather Station

The next step was to build my own weather station. Using scrap pieces of wood, I created a little box with louvered sides for ventilation. I placed two thermometers inside—a regular dry-bulb type and a "wet bulb" thermometer, which is created by putting a shoelace dipped in water over the bulb (the wet bulb reading is cooler due to evaporation). Humidity can be calculated by comparing the difference between the dry and wet bulb readings. I also made a "hair hygrometer" out of a piece of my sister's blond hair. Hair contracts and becomes a little thicker and shorter when it is humid, especially fine blond hair. By attaching a pointer and a dial to the hair, you can make a humidity gauge.

My weather box went out in the backyard on a post. Later I built a wind vane and anemometer to keep track of the winds. Three times each day I checked all the weather observations and kept them in a notebook. To this day, I still have the instrument shelter and all my weather records from over twenty-five years ago.

By the time I was in high school, I knew that I wanted to be a television meteorologist. I watched all the local stations for weather and usually preferred forecasts that called for lots of snow or a severe storm. (This is not uncommon among "weather nuts" —we're always excited about approaching storms. Quiet, sunny weather is boring!) In high school, two events had a major impact on my future career in meteorology. The University of Wisconsin in Madison is one of the largest schools for meteorology in the nation. In the mid-1970s, Dr. Frank Sechrist was a professor of synoptic meteorology at the university. In addition to teaching his students how to forecast weather, Dr. Sechrist was interested in television weather. This was a little unusual at the time, as most folks in meteorological circles felt that television was beneath them. Dr. Sechrist, however, did weather reports and short educational programs on the public television channel, which I enjoyed watching.

Weather forecasters rely upon information gathered from instruments such as weather balloons and radiosondes (above) and solar-powered weather stations (below).

Dr. Frank, as he was more familiarly called, was also a hiker, and some of his long hikes were featured on television. He was on a very long hike from Madison to Lake Superior when my parents happened to meet him. They were driving along, saw Frank walking by the side of the road, and decided to stop and offer him a drink. Well, Dr. Frank was very pleased to have the cold refreshment, and as a token of gratitude, he offered to show me around the meteorology department when he got back. It was quite a thrill for this wide-eyed high school freshman to be escorted around the university weather department by his TV hero!

Terry Kelly

The next coincidence that had a huge impact on my career had to do with ice cream. I worked in a Baskin-Robbins ice cream store during my junior and senior years in high school. Terry Kelly, one of Dr. Frank's graduate students, had become the local weather forecaster on the ABC-affiliated station in Madison—WKOW TV (that's K-O-W as in COW, because Wisconsin is the dairy state). Anyway, Mr. Kelly had a sweet tooth, and he liked to stop in for a scoop of Jamoca ice cream before going to the station for the late news. I always gave him an extra big scoop—and then would try to say something intelligent about the weather. We became friends, and then one day my father gave me some advice. "Mike," he said, "you're always waiting on this guy. Why don't you ask him if he could use some help at the TV station?" Being a teenager, I said, "Aw, Dad, that's a stupid idea!" But of course it was a pretty smart idea, and I finally got up the courage to ask Mr. Kelly if he needed an enthusiastic helper. Fortunately he said yes, and I started out at the station by helping answer phones and hanging up maps. I worked at the station for almost ten years, working my way from being an office helper to eventually becoming the number-two weathercaster behind Terry Kelly. I was thankful for my father's advice!

Mike Nelson's very first television broadcast on WKOW, July 4, 1979.

So that's how I got into the television business. After ten years at WKOW, I moved to St. Louis, Missouri, and KMOX-TV. I stayed there for six years before coming to KUSA in Denver in 1991. Along the way, I've witnessed tremendous changes in the way that we prepare and present the television weather reports you see every day. *(Continued on page 94)*

> I have witnessed tremendous changes in the way that we prepare and present television weather reports.

Mike Nelson Says: Build Your Own Home Weather Station

Colorado's changeable weather can be spellbinding to any sky watcher, but kids are often especially enthralled. To help kids learn more about weather, Mike Nelson suggests building your own weather station.

It's not difficult to do. As a child, Nelson made his own station out of scrap wood following instructions from a Time Life book. Begin by building a rectangular box about 12 to 18 inches square with louvers (movable slats) on the sides for ventilation. Paint the box white to reflect heat away from your station so that your readings will be accurate.

The first instrument you'll want is easy to find in any hardware store: a thermometer. While you're at it, get two of them. You will use the first one for reading the temperature, but cover the bulb of the second one with a small, wet piece of cloth (even a shoelace will work!). This wet bulb thermometer will be cooler than the dry bulb thermometer due to evaporation. Comparing the difference between the thermometers will help you calculate the humidity in the air.

Although you may want to purchase a barometer, other instruments are just as easy to build yourself. Make a rain gauge out of an old can or bottle and add your own calibrations to the side. Wind vanes can be crafted out of wood; just be sure the vane can move with the wind. To measure the force and speed of winds, build an anemometer out of thin pieces of plastic, a roller skate wheel, and a few plastic cups (see illustration). Need a more sophisticated way to gauge humidity? You can construct a hygrometer using a piece of hair attached to a dial with a pointer.

You could also buy a home weather station at an electronics store, complete with instruments that will feed information into your home computer. But if you ask Mike Nelson, he'll tell you he enjoyed building his own station and recording his observations in a journal by hand. "To this day, I still have the instrument shelter and all my weather records from over 25 years ago," he says.

Anemometer

Find a skateboard or rollerskate wheel (or any type of pivot with 360° movement) and nail it to the top of a 6-foot pole, like a tomato stake. The wheel should be parallel to the ground so that it spins easily. Fashion a cross from two foot-long dowels and attach plastic or paper cups to the ends.

Wind Vane

On another pole with a wheel mounted on top, glue a wind vane made of balsam wood to the wheel. The wind vane will show you which way the wind is blowing.

Rain Gauge

Place an empty jar on top of your weather box. Add your own calibrations to the side. Empty each day.

Weather Box

Build a wooden box with side slats for ventilation and a door to enclose the weather instruments inside. Paint the box white and mount it on a pole about 4 feet from the ground (white reflects heat away from the box).

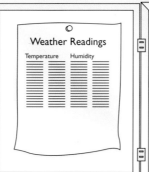

Temperature and Humidity

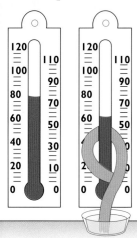

Mount two thermometers side by side. Use the first one, the dry bulb thermometer, to read the temperature. For the second one, have a shoelace or piece of cloth wrap around the bulb and go down into a small container of water. The wet bulb thermometer will be cooler due to evaporation. Comparing the difference between the two thermometers will help you calculate the humidity.

Hair Hygrometer

Build a small base. Attach a pointer to it so it can tilt up and down. Tie strands of human hair (blonde hair works best) to the pointer. Attach the strands to an overhang above. Draw a chart to mount on the wall behind the pointer. When the air is humid the hair contracts and moves the pointer down. The hair extends when the air is dry.

Teletype machines

I learned a lot about weather forecasting when I had to prepare dozens of different forecasts each day.

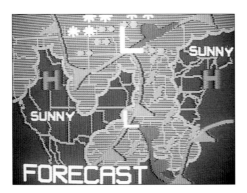

The main challenge in the 1950s up through the 1970s was to come up with a way to display basic meteorological information in a manner that would be easy enough for the audience to understand. This was usually accomplished by taking raw weather data from teletype and facsimile machines, simplifying it, and then displaying the information on a big map on the wall. A giant mural of the United States was painted on a wall of the studio, and hooks, magnets, and greasepaint were used to designate weather features. Some stations tried to be more creative by putting the map on a glass wall and having the weathercaster stand behind the glass and draw the weather LIVE. Unfortunately, this required not only art skill, but also the ability to draw backwards!

Terry Kelly was quite a visionary and entrepreneur. About the time that I began to work for him, he started a weather consulting company called Weather Central. This private weather firm provided forecasts for radio stations, highway departments, agribusiness, and ski areas that needed specialized weather information that the short-staffed National Weather Service could not offer. I learned a lot about weather forecasting in a big hurry when I had to prepare dozens of different forecasts each day.

Computer Graphics and Weather

In 1979, Terry Kelly teamed up with Dr. Richard Daly, a professor of computer science at the University of Wisconsin, to begin a new venture—computerized weather graphics for television. Other people around the country had tried to use computers to generate weather maps, but with little success due to the high cost of hardware and the undeveloped stage of software. Kelly and Daly formed a company called "ColorGraphics Weather Systems," with initial systems based upon some of the computer display breakthroughs at the University of Wisconsin's Department of Space Science and Engineering. A system had been developed there called McIdas—an acronym for Man-Computer Interactive Data System. The McIdas system used a large mainframe computer to allow meteorologists to draw and analyze satellite cloud data directly on a computer screen. By today's standards, it was like

"Space Invaders," but at the time it was the cutting edge. The McIdas system was designed for use in research and National Weather Service forecasting, but unfortunately it was too expensive for a television station.

Terry Kelly and Richard Daly envisioned creating a weather computer system that would be easy to use and affordable. The first ColorGraphics system was based upon an Apple 2C computer and could generate five different color choices on a black background. Map resolution was blocky, fonts were hard to read, and because the system couldn't be plugged directly into the TV station's routing switcher, a camera had to be aimed at a monitor to get the image on television. Despite these problems, the first ColorGraphics computer sold like hotcakes!

My job with ColorGraphics was to install the computers at television stations and train the local weathercasters in how to use them. By the early 1980s, I was traveling around the nation with the weather computers, doing local TV weather reports in Madison

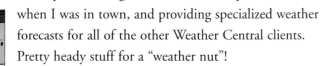

when I was in town, and providing specialized weather forecasts for all of the other Weather Central clients. Pretty heady stuff for a "weather nut"!

One of my stops on the weather computer trail was Channel 9 in Denver, which then was KBTV. That was in 1982, and I brought the latest version of the ColorGraphics system, the Liveline 3. I installed the computer and trained Bill Kuster and Stormy Rottman on how to use it. This was a great thrill for me—Stormy was one of the legends of television weather around the nation. He had been in the Denver market since the early 1970s, and not only did he have a way of explaining the weather in common language, but he was warm and approachable. People said watching him was like watching your favorite uncle do the weather on television. I felt honored to train Stormy, even if he wasn't sure if he wanted to learn this "new-fangled computer."

Fortunately, on this particular trip, my wife Cindy was allowed to come along and she talked Stormy into learning the system by challenging him. "Stormy," she said, "I'm not even a meteorologist,

Stormy Rottman

95

and I can figure out how to run this thing!" Bill Kuster was also brand-new to the concept of a weather computer. Bill had come to 9NEWS in 1979, after a long and successful career in Philadelphia, where he anchored the weather on a news team that featured Jessica Savitch and Tom Snyder. The team there had been hugely popular, but Bill and his wife, Dot, eventually decided to move to the Rocky Mountains. To this day Bill remains a good friend, and Stormy will always be one of my personal heroes. Cindy and I enjoyed our trip to Denver and 9NEWS so much that we decided that this was where we wanted to live if we ever had the chance. Fortunately, that chance arrived. Bill and Dot refer to Denver as "The Kusters' Last Stand"—I guess that holds for the Nelsons as well!

So, You Want to be a Meteorologist

Kids who love to watch the skies are always asking meteorologist Mike Nelson one important question: How can I become a meteorologist?

Start studying weather early and apply yourself, advises Nelson. "I decided to study meteorology by the time I was in junior high school," he says, adding that working on your skills in mathematics as well as in physics and chemistry in high school will make it that much easier to get into a meteorology program in college.

Nelson, who received his bachelor's degree in the field from the University of Wisconsin, notes that institutions offering degrees in meteorology usually require three semesters of calculus, two semesters of physics, and two semesters of chemistry. Once these basic courses are completed, students dig into "core" classes in thermodynamics, dynamics, synoptics, climatology, and tropical meteorology, as well as classes devoted to storm forecasting and instruction for weather-prediction instruments.

Having been in the television weather-forecasting industry since his days as a meteorologist at WKOW-TV in Madison, Nelson tells prospective broadcast meteorologists that the field is somewhat limited. "There are only about 600 TV stations that do news and weather across the country," he notes, adding that anyone planning to become a media meteorologist should take a few communications or acting classes as well. A little homework couldn't hurt, either. "I used to practice in front of a mirror," Nelson remembers. "It helped me get over being nervous."

All that preparation must have paid off—Nelson has won five Heartland Regional Emmys from the National Association of Television Arts and Sciences for his work at KUSA-TV in Denver, where he joined the weather staff in 1991. Broadcasting daily weather reports at 5, 6, and 10 P.M., Nelson enjoys the challenges Colorado's unpredictable weather often poses to meteorologists. "Probably the best thing about the job is trying to forecast the weather in the mountains, as the tough terrain creates many different kinds of storms," Nelson tells kids. With that comes a need to accept that, well, sometimes the weather here changes so quickly that it's almost impossible to predict. "Most of the time we are correct on the forecast," he says, "so people don't get too mad at us."

Weather computers, just like calculators and personal computers, continued to grow in power and shrink in cost. They're still not cheap—many of the systems used by television stations tally into six figures—but they've become the mainstay of the television weather business. If you travel around the country, it's very rare to find anyone using an old weather board for even a small part of the weathercast.

Of course now we have all sorts of fancy things we can do with computers, including time lapse, lightning detection, Doppler radar, and "fly through" animations. Time lapse is actually not new; Dr. Sechrist and Terry Kelly both used an old Bolex film camera to take a single frame of film every ten to thirty seconds. This film had to be rushed out to be developed in time for the nightly weather reports. Today, our weather computer simply grabs a single frame off one of our weather cameras every few seconds and stores it for playback. Now it takes almost no time at all to do a time-lapse display. I enjoy not only time lapsing the clouds and sunsets, but also focusing the camera on highways, skiers, construction equipment, window washers, or anything else that might be fun to see in high-speed motion.

Lightning Detection

Lightning detection is fascinating to most viewers. In 1982, I installed the first lightning detecting system at 9NEWS. This system has been modernized considerably in the past fifteen years, but it still remains a mainstay of our summertime weather arsenal. One of

the interesting things about lightning is that it will sometimes begin well ahead of the precipitation in a thunderstorm. Since weather radar "sees" only precipitation, the lightning detector can provide a ten- to twenty-minute advance notice about developing thunderstorms. We occasionally see lightning even in the wintertime. Cold-season lightning is indicative of a large amount of turbulence in the atmosphere and is a sign that heavy snow squalls may be developing.

Weather Radar

Radar is one of the "big guns" of television weather. Many years ago, weather radar was very crude, basically just a camera pointed at a glowing electron tube display with a slowly fading sweep line that looked like something from an old war movie. In the mid-1970s, these radar displays were replaced by the biggest innovation of the time, "Color Radar." Each intensity level for the precipitation (light to heavy) is assigned a different color, and usually light blue or green marks the light showers while the heavy downpours are shown in orange or red. The radar works by sending out a burst of microwave energy, similar in frequency to your microwave oven. At this particular wavelength (about five to ten centimeters), the energy tends to pass through clouds but bounce or echo off of rain, snow, or hail. By timing the signal from when it leaves the radar to when it bounces back, we can calculate the location of the precipitation. This "conventional" radar has actually been around since World War II, and its technology is basically the same whether it is displayed with the old circular greenish scope of the 1950s or the colorized version of the 1970s.

In the 1980s, technology made another jump with the introduction of Doppler weather radar. Doppler radar not only "sees" precipitation, but it can also "see" the wind. Of course, wind is invisible, but the Doppler radar can analyze the movement of raindrops and snowflakes inside the cloud. Those cloud particles are blown about by wind, and by observing those particles we can see how fast the winds are blowing and in what direction. Doppler is actually the name of a nineteenth-century Dutch physicist, Christian Doppler, who first formally described a phenomenon with which we are all familiar. If you've ever noticed how the sound from an approaching car or train changes as it passes by, then you have experienced the "Doppler Shift." As the vehicle moves closer to you, sound waves from the car or train are picked up by your ear. Because the object is moving toward you, the sound waves tend to "bunch up" and the frequency increases. That's why the tone or pitch seems to rise as the car or train gets closer. When it passes by, the sound waves are still coming from the vehicle toward your ear, but because it is moving away, the sound waves are farther apart. The frequency is lower and consequently the pitch drops. The

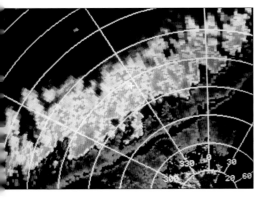

A Doppler radar image of a cold front.

faster the object approaches and moves by, the greater the change in pitch or frequency. We can measure this change to get a good idea of how fast an object is moving.

The Doppler Shift works with sound waves or with microwaves. With radar, we send a large number of pulses of radar (or microwave energy) out from the radar antenna. Those signals bounce off an object and return to the radar at slightly different times, depending on whether the object is moving toward or away from the radar antenna. The measurement of this shift in the frequency of the radar return signals helps us determine how fast the object is moving toward or away from the radar. Doppler radar has many uses—including law enforcement. Police use Doppler radar to catch speeding motorists. It's also the way we determine the speed of a baseball pitch or a hockey slap shot.

In weather forecasting, Doppler radar provides two major improvements over conventional weather radar. First, it eliminates

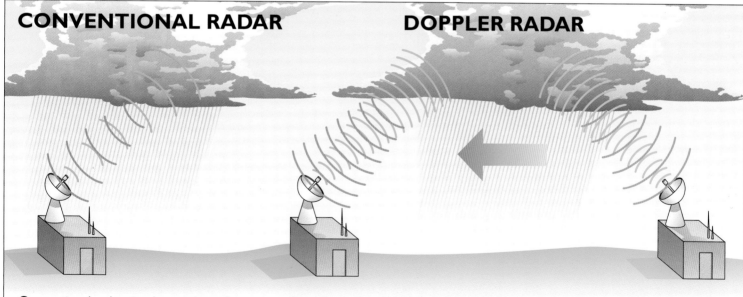

CONVENTIONAL RADAR

DOPPLER RADAR

Conventional radar signals pass through clouds but reflect off of rain, snow, or hail. Location and distance can be determined by timing the return of the reflected radar signals.

Doppler radar sends out more signals very quickly. These reflected signals show not only precipitation but also movement of the precipitation. This movement provides information on wind currents and speeds, which allows detection of windshears and tornadoes. As a storm approaches, reflected radar signals increase in frequency, and they decrease as a storm moves away.

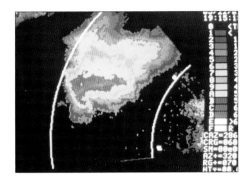

most of the confusing false echoes that used to clutter up the radar screen. Older radars had a problem with the signal bouncing off buildings and trees and sending back the impression that there was precipitation in those locations. This was very misleading to the television viewer. Additionally, the actual precipitation area was "caught in the clutter" and consequently was very hard to see. Doppler radar eliminates ground clutter by noting only moving objects. If a building stays in the same place long enough, the clutter suppression program in the radar computer simply eliminates the echo. Nevertheless, little bits of clutter can occur on a Doppler display if the signal inadvertently bounces off other moving objects. For example, that little tiny pixel of green on radar might be a bird flying by your house!

The biggest benefit of Doppler weather radar is that it allows us to have "X-ray vision" to peer into the heart of severe thunderstorms. Determining how rain and hail are blown around inside a storm allows us to look for areas of very strong winds and possible

tornadoes. The Doppler enables us to find places in a storm cloud where the winds are blowing very rapidly in one direction and nearby blowing very rapidly in the opposite direction. These areas contain what meteorologists call a "shear." The greater the shear, the better the chance that a tornado or downburst may be forming. By using Doppler radar, we can pinpoint these areas much earlier than ever before. The result is earlier, better, and more useful tornado and severe thunderstorm warnings. More advance notice can save lives!

Doppler radar became available for television in the early 1980s. By the beginning of the 1990s, most television stations in larger cities were equipped with their own Dopplers. These radars are not cheap—most installations cost between one hundred fifty and three hundred thousand dollars. That's part of the reason that television stations always come up with such fancy names for their radar. After making such a large investment, the station management wants to get the most for their money, so they come up with important sounding names: Super Doppler, Double

Doppler, Doppler 2000, Doppler Max, SkyWarn Doppler, Storm Scan Doppler, and the like. All the Doppler radars used around the nation are excellent—some have more features than others, but the upshot is that the competition between television stations ultimately benefits the viewer. If each station has an excellent radar display, the viewer has more choices and better weather information in the event of dangerous weather.

In the past few years, there have been a few improvements in Doppler radar, particularly with how information is displayed. Until recently, the center of the radar sweep marked the center of the radar map. This worked well if the radar was located in the middle of town. If the radar was located somewhere else, the audience could be confused by thinking the middle of the map was the center of town, when actually it was simply the radar site. New computer technology has allowed us to remap the radar echoes onto any size or scale map. The most interesting part of this improvement is that it allows us to remap the radar onto a very small map—right down to the city streets. We can now show a thunderstorm cell that literally is raining on one side of the street and not on the other. This close-up mapping is very helpful with the type of small, fast-moving storms we have in Colorado. The very latest software allows us to click on the radar screen and actually have the name of the street pop up. Similarly, we can click on a storm cell, type in its speed and direction, and have the radar calculate what cities will be affected by the storm and at what time. This "storm path analyzer" function is very useful with long-track squall lines and has provided important advance notice of approaching severe thunderstorms and tornadoes around the country.

Police use Doppler radar to catch speeding motorists. It's also the way we determine the speed of a baseball pitch or a hockey slap shot.

3-D Weather

In the early 1990s, another important development occurred in TV weather graphics, fly-through weather. The first 3-D weather system was marketed by a friend of mine, Paul Douglas, the former

chief meteorologist at KARE-TV in Minneapolis. KARE is a sister station to KUSA, and Paul was one of the first users of the earliest ColorGraphics systems. Using a powerful Silicon Graphics platform, Paul and his programmers developed a system that mapped the weather over a three-dimensional background. This allowed the user to change vantage points, elevation, and angle, and observe the weather from many different perspectives. The computer had to be powerful enough to draw the map background, topography, and the weather very quickly, because the basic idea was to start at a certain viewpoint (say, right over the foothills west of Denver) and then "fly" across the country. The computer would then inter-polate between the starting point and the end point and render an animation, graphic frame by graphic frame. Think of it as the cyber equivalent of drawing a stick figure on a set of flash cards and changing the position of the figure slightly on each card. Then, when you flip through the cards quickly, you get the illusion of the figure moving.

9NEWS became a test site for Douglas's first 3-D system, called "EarthWatch." The EarthWatch system took a little getting used to; the early flights were pretty wild. We had to tone down our enthusiasm for "zooming" through the weather because the audience found it difficult to follow. That might be an understatement—we received a few complaints that we were actually making our viewers nauseated! Rather than doling out Dramamine, we opted to tone down the fast spins and quick turns.

Over the past six or seven years, we've learned to use the fly-around capability much more effectively. Now, we often fly gently from one part of the country to another and animate a particular weather feature. Three-dimensional weather has become the biggest breakthrough in television weather graphics of this decade, and most weathercasters around the country now use it to some degree.

The Blue Screen

The one aspect of the television weather report that still surprises most people is the fact that we do not actually stand in front of the weather map. When you see me on your television set at home, it looks like I'm standing in front of a giant weather map. But if you were standing in the 9NEWS Backyard, it would look completely different. You would see the camera about ten feet in front of me as I stood talking and pointing, but behind me there would not be a weather map. All you would see is a great big blue wall. If you didn't know what was going on, you might think I was losing my mind! I stand there and discuss the heat in Denver and point—but there is no Denver to point to, just the blue wall. What we are using is something called "Chroma-Key." This type of special effect or "TV magic" works very simply—the camera "sees" me and it "sees" the blue wall. We've set up the camera in a special way so that wherever the camera "sees" blue, it makes it look like a weather map at home on your TV.

Now, since all there is behind me is a blue wall, how do I know what to point at? In the 9Backyard, we have a television set in a corner off-camera. I basically do the same thing that you do:

I watch Mike Nelson on television! Except for me it's a little strange being in front of the camera and watching myself on television at the same time—it's almost like talking into a mirror. When I want to talk about hot weather in Denver, I stick my hand out into thin air, turn and look at myself on the screen, and then move my hand around until it looks like I'm pointing at Denver to all of you

at home. It's a little bit like patting your head and rubbing your stomach at the same time! I've been doing Chroma-Key for a long time (nearly twenty years), so I usually know where to point. But the first time you try it, you think you're pointing right at Denver, and then you look and realize you're actually pointing to Hawaii!

One other interesting aspect of Chroma-Key is that it limits your wardrobe. You can't wear certain shades of blue! If you were to wear the same color blue as the background, the camera would see the blue color of your suit, and it would make it look like the weather map! You'd literally be "wearing the weather"—cold fronts down your arm, snow on your belly, and sunshine on your back!

Navy is okay, as well as very light blue shirts, but you won't see a medium-blue suit on anyone in the 9Backyard. Green can be used instead of blue for the Chroma-Key, but it's not practical for us because the leaves on the trees in the 9 Backyard would have little weather maps on them.

You may have noticed the little "clicker" that we hold in our hand while doing the weather. It's actually a garage-door opener that our engineers rigged up to change the weather map. When we hit the button, the signal goes to the weather computer and tells it to jump to the next map. I also wonder if it doesn't open somebody's garage down the street!

You may also have wondered about the little "hearing aid" gadget we wear in our ears, called an IFB or program interrupt. Basically just a little walkie-talkie, the IFB allows people in the control room to give us instructions. The producer and director of the newscast often need to tell us things like how much time we have left; for example, "one minute, thirty seconds, wrap it up." They can also provide information about breaking news or technical problems. ("Mike, the tape machine just ate your time lapse!") Our producers and directors don't tell us what to say about the weather, but they do talk to us frequently during the weather report.

It takes about an hour of preparing forecasts and graphics for each minute that we are on the air. When I go on television, I laugh and joke with Ed Sardella and Adele Arakawa, get up from the news desk, and then walk about thirty feet to the back door. I quickly don my hat, gloves, and coat (assuming it's cold or snowy), and go out the door, talking about the weather the entire time. I go to the map wall and point at something that's not really there. I have to remember where it's hot, cold, raining, snowing, and where the weather patterns are moving. I need to click the button at the right time and keep track of what map will come up next. Try doing all of this in about three minutes while someone is talking in your ear! And that doesn't even include getting the forecast right!

I'm not trying to drum up sympathy—it's a great job and I love it. But I do want to emphasize that the weather is the only part of a newscast that *predicts* rather than *reports.* To a viewing audience, there may be a big difference between a snowstorm and sunshine, but meteorologically it may have been just a slight

change in the storm track. My weather report always agrees with the other television channels when we show the high and low temperatures for the day. Those numbers are facts. But our job is much more like that of a stockbroker. If you ask five different brokers for details about the stock market, you'll likely get five different forecasts. When people ask, "We can land on the moon—why can't we predict the weather?" I answer, "Because it's easier to land on the moon." A mission to the moon is a matter of propulsion and supplies. Take enough rocket fuel, food, and oxygen, and you should be able to get there and back. Weather forecasting involves figuring out how a massive nuclear reactor nearly 100 million miles away will affect a complex mix of gases on a swirling, irregularly shaped planet. In addition to the rotation, throw in factors like huge bodies of water that can store vast amounts of heat and release it into the atmosphere. Also change the axis of the spinning planet so that different parts of the surface get more heat than others at different times of year. The result is a churning witch's brew of clouds and storms that we try to track and project into the future.

We'll never get to the level that will allow us to pinpoint the exact weather for a day weeks in advance. We are, however, getting much better at nailing down short-term severe weather events and predicting the general trends for an entire season. Improvements in both areas can save lives and tremendous amounts of money by providing valuable advance notice of local events like tornadoes or hailstorms and long-term episodes such as El Niño.

In television weather, we serve many masters. We try to provide accurate and timely information in a lively and fun-to-watch manner. We try to cover the local scene, but also give people all over the state of Colorado the information they need. We attempt to give an overview of national weather and also educate the viewer about important events in weather history or new research about the greenhouse effect or ozone depletion. We could probably fill at least five to eight minutes of news time each night, but news and sports have plenty to say as well, so we do what we can with the time allotted. The phone lines and e-mail box are always open if you have a suggestion on how we can make the weather more relevant to your life.

> **When people ask, "We can land on the moon — why can't we predict the weather?" I answer, "Because it's easier to land on the moon."**

Photographing WEATHER
by John Fielder

A review of the basics by Colorado's foremost landscape photographer, John Fielder.

For the most part, our skies in Colorado define the current weather. Blue skies are often the product of high pressure; gray skies mean low pressure. Cumulus clouds and lightning tell us what time of the year it is; rainbows and pink clouds are clues about the time of day. So to the visually oriented photographer, skies and weather are one and the same.

Most people think of me as a landscape photographer and forget that I photograph skies almost as often as I do places. Scenic compositions that contain a horizon always have land and sky. Therefore I pay attention to techniques necessary to make good photographs of skies.

Here are a few tips that might help you to create better photographs of weather and skies.

Composition of Sky and Landscape (easy)

In most cases I avoid putting the horizon in the middle of the picture. This creates symmetrical balance that is perceived by our brains as boring. In my photographs, I like to catch the viewer's attention quickly with a dominant feature. This can be a conspicuous object, like a single cloud in a large sky, but it could also be the whole sky or the whole landscape above or below the horizon. When pink clouds dominate a dark, featureless landscape, I compose two-thirds sky, one-third landscape. When the landscape is more interesting, I do the opposite.

Adding Dominant Features to a Sky (easy)

Even photographs with asymmetrical balance can be boring. When the sky does not contain dramatic clouds or colors, I often add a dominant feature such as the silhouette of a tree. A tree without leaves allows the intricate pattern of branches to be more conspicuous. I make photographs like this at sunrise or sunset when the sun doesn't shine on the landscape and tree, which is also when skies are most colorful. Because the sky is so much brighter than a tree in shadow, the tree will appear black in the photograph. This makes any silhouetted dominant feature, even statues or buildings, very conspicuous against the sky.

Photographing Rainbows (easy)

I prefer that a rainbow rise from the ground in a photograph; therefore, I always include the horizon and remember my rule about composition. How else would one find that pot of gold? Rainbows always seem to occur in bright situations, whether the sky is dark or light. Light meters in cameras perceive this and always decrease the exposure in order to keep the colors saturated. So most cameras, including "point and shoots" (and even disposables) will make great pictures of rainbows without hard work on your part. For you advanced photographers, don't use a polarizing filter—it will make the rainbow disappear!

Photographing Lightning (more advanced)

Unless you can predict the future (in which case I'd like to go to Central City with you) and know when lightning will flash, you must use time exposures to photograph lightning. That is, you need to set up your camera on a sturdy tripod and open the shutter for as long as it takes to catch a flash. Most point-and-shoots don't allow time exposures. The longer your exposure, the more flashes you are apt to record. It's easier to photograph lightning at night than it is during daytime thunderstorms. At night there's no chance to overexpose the landscape in the scene. During the day, small apertures must be employed in order to allow long exposures.

Photographing in Bad Weather (any level)

My best photographs of what I call "unique moments in time," or moments that may never occur in exactly the same way again in a million years, usually result from bad weather. Intense sunsets and rainbows tend to occur after thunderstorms, especially in the Colorado mountains. My "sherpas," the people who help me backpack into wilderness, don't like it when they hear me praying for bad weather in the tent each night—they prefer to work in good weather! Be prepared to brave wind, rain, and snow at any time of the year in Colorado. Keep cameras dry in ziplock bags, but take them out when it's time to shoot. And be very careful about lightning. It is unpredictable, can literally come out of the "blue," and is especially dangerous on mountains above timberline. And metal tripods and cameras attract it!

Great cloud! More landscape, or avoiding the lights and building, would emphasize the cloud more. **Sylvia Lujan**

Excellent composition. The silhouetted trees are very effective. **Ronald Coil**

Channel Nine Viewers Look to the Sky

with comments by John Fielder

Terrific color and contrast! I love the moon, too. **Jack Weust**

Beautiful diffraction of white light. Power lines sometimes create an unnecessary diversion.

Gordon Copley

Great cloud! Perhaps move it left or right a bit to give the photo more asymmetry. **Dewayne Fenton**

Excellent shot of sunset or sunrise. I'd like to see a bit more of the trees and their shapes.

Andrea Ferency

The road sign works well in this scene. Interesting counterpoint to the "natural" sky.

Terry Williford

Great sunset or sunrise! Lowering the horizon a bit would show more sky.

Jack and Marie Lawson

I love the silhouette of the posts. Good composition overall. Just the right amount of sky and landscape.

Nancy Schara

Very dramatic shot! Lower the horizon a bit to create asymmetrical balance.

Bonnie Handy

Ken Stevenson

Dave Platt

The Rocky Mountains are major players in Colorado weather. As winds blow over the mountains, air is forced to move up, over, and around the rough terrain. During the warm months, rising air often forms into thunderstorms as the moisture condenses out as the air cools. Sometimes these storms become stalled over the mountains and create flash-flood conditions.

During the colder months, high, fast-moving winds bounce and churn their way over the mountains. These winds react to the rugged terrain much like the water in a mountain stream. Standing waves and whirlpools of air develop "downstream" from the mountains. Moisture trapped in these waves of air create clouds that are whipped and sculpted into flying saucer shapes called **lenticular** clouds.

Another reason to live in Colorado! Our sunsets and sunrises have an orange glow due to the increased scattering of the longer yellow, orange, and red light. This scattering is due to the larger amount of dust the sunlight travels through when the sun is near the horizon.

Mark Knox

The bubble-shaped **cumulonimbus mammatus** clouds are ominous but not dangerous in themselves. These bulbous protuberances are caused by rain-cooled air sinking beneath the anvil of the storm. Mammatus clouds are eerie looking but are merely "special effects" added to make a thunderstorm look menacing.

Paul Lambert

The early morning sky sets these high-level **cirrus** clouds ablaze. Increasing cirrus clouds can be a sign of an approaching storm; hence the old saying, "Red sky at morning, sailors take warning."

Barbara Larson

George Chenoweth

The iridescent glow of these clouds is sometimes called **mother of pearl.** High-altitude cirrus clouds are made of tiny ice crystals. These crystals bend the light rays that pass through them, much like a prism does. This bending or refraction of the light creates the rainbow colors.

When these building clouds, called **cumulus congestus,** begin to grow high in the sky, thunderstorms are usually not far behind.

Charles Gadway

The dramatic sunbeams that stream out from the setting sun are called **crepuscular rays.** They are caused by clouds and mountains casting intermittent shadows onto the sunlit background. Dust and haze create the beam effect. The rays are actually parallel, but appear to converge in the same way that railroad tracks appear to come together in the distance.

Jay Gustafson

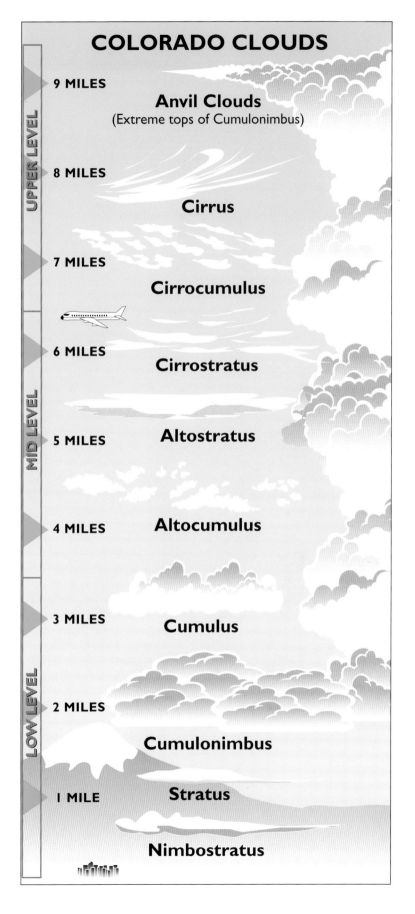

COLORADO CLOUDS

UPPER LEVEL

9 MILES

Anvil Clouds
(Extreme tops of Cumulonimbus)

8 MILES

Cirrus

7 MILES

Cirrocumulus

6 MILES

Cirrostratus

MID LEVEL

5 MILES

Altostratus

4 MILES

Altocumulus

3 MILES

Cumulus

LOW LEVEL

2 MILES

Cumulonimbus

1 MILE

Stratus

Nimbostratus

Videotaping Dramatic Weather
Practical Tips from Eric Kehe, 9NEWS Photographer

Taking effective videos of dramatic or even violent weather is more than being in the right place at the right time—it's a combination of understanding how a storm works and knowing what to do when it counts. Despite the excitement of chasing a storm or tornado, safety first must always be the rule. Beyond that, there are some key points you should keep in mind that can improve the quality of your home weather videos.

My love of stormy weather goes back to when I was a kid. I grew up in the Chicago suburbs, and one evening, when I was about five years old, an amazing thing happened

to me and my family. Mom was cooking supper, and I was playing in the living room with four of my brothers and sisters. Because we lived in the flatlands, we could watch as storms rolled in from miles away. But this day—April 21, 1967—was different. The sky looked odd and the low-hanging clouds were an ominous greenish-black

color. As we stood at the living room window and watched, a tornado formed right before our eyes. We ran for the crawl space to be safe, but thought there was surely no chance a tornado could hit our house. We sat hunched in the dark for several minutes waiting for the storm to pass, but it didn't. It hit—hard. It was the loudest noise I'd ever heard. I remember screaming in pain, not because of the noise, but because my ears wanted to burst from the change in pressure. The noise and chaos seemed to go on forever.

When the storm finally passed, our house was destroyed. The walls were blown out and shattered glass lay everywhere. The damage was extensive throughout the area; 58 people died in that one storm (fortunately, my family was safe). We rebuilt our home, but the next year my father moved us to the mountains of Colorado. He could not bear the thought of our experiencing another tornado.

That day, although frightening, was probably the most thrilling day of my life. In fact, it was so exciting that I've been trying to recapture that feeling ever since. When I became a news photographer at 9NEWS, I took it as a challenge to try to capture a tornado on videotape. I wanted to share my experience of seeing an actual tornado with my viewers.

On May 30, 1996, I unexpectedly got my chance. Kathy Sabine, a weather anchor at 9NEWS, and I had been called out on a storm chase. What began as a relatively routine news story turned into an unprecedented event. Just outside the town of Fort Morgan, Kathy and I saw not only one but two tornadoes forming and touching down—at the same time! (We called them "sister twisters.") I captured them both on tape, and fortunately no one was hurt. The excitement was back!

For years now, I've made a hobby of trying to understand storms and figuring out the best way to videotape them. Here are some things I look for when I'm trying to take pictures of tornadoes or any dramatic weather activity. Remember, usually luck plays just as strong a role as anything else—but if you understand even a little bit about tornadoes and storms in general, you can greatly improve your chances of creating a really great video. Keep the following tips in mind.

1. SAFETY FIRST. The most important thing is to always know where you are in relationship to the storm and which way it's moving. If the storm is headed your direction, get out of harm's way! This means that before you even enter the area, you need to have a plan about how to get in and out safely. Firefighters call it an escape route. Is your vehicle gassed up and running properly? Do you have proper maps? Have you identified all the roads to get you in and out of the area quickly in case something goes wrong? Be sure to plan ahead.

2. BACK OFF. Get to a vantage point where you can see and anticipate the storm. Remember, you can't take pictures if you're stuck inside the system and have zero visibility—and you can't take pictures if you're getting blasted with hail. Look for a safe and clear position that's free of obstructions like buildings and telephone poles. Don't let yourself get carried away by excitement—a shot looking straight into the vortex of a tornado might look cool, but you probably won't live to share it with anyone.

3. APPROACH THE SOUTHWEST CORNER OF THE CELL. Based on my experience, this is usually where a tornado will form. A southwest position is very important for three reasons: 1) you can see wall clouds as they form; 2) you can see signs of rotation; 3) you're in a good position to shoot the corner of the storm.

To create a good video of a tornado, it's important to have contrast. The tornado must stand out from the rest of the background— a gray tornado against a gray background doesn't make for a picture of a tornado at all. Angle yourself so that you can shoot across the southwest corner of the storm. This allows you to obtain the cleanest image of the tornado by separating the funnel from the background through varying contrast and color.

4. HOLD YOUR SHOT. Don't freak out and swish, pan, and zoom. Think about shooting video the same way you compose a still photograph. Frame it, compose it, and roll your tape for fifteen seconds. Then zoom in, change your angle, and compose your next shot. Roll for another fifteen seconds. If you have a great shot, keep rolling tape. (If you're shooting a cow flying through the air, hold that shot until it's over!)

One of the best parts of seeing a tornado on videotape is what you hear, from the sounds of nature in its wildest moments to how people react to what they're seeing. If you're not hearing any interesting natural sounds, talk away. Give yourself a play-by-play running dialogue and try to capture the excitement of the moment. The goal is to shoot steady, sequenced video with meaningful natural sound.

5. LAST BUT NOT LEAST—PROTECT YOUR CAMERA. Try to shoot under the overhang of a building or under the hatchback of your car where you're protected from the elements. Purchase a rain cover or some sort of plastic protective garb for your camera. You may get a great shot by dashing out and braving the elements, but if you trash your camera, you'll never be able to do it again.

The Fragile PLANET

Nov 97
0ft
300ft
600ft

The comment I most often hear when discussing the topic of long-term climate change is: "You guys can barely forecast tomorrow's weather, let alone the weather for the next hundred years!" Although it's painful to admit, to a certain extent that comment rings true. The weather forecast is amazingly complex day to day, let alone over the course of decades. In the past twenty-five years, we've gone from worrying about the imminent arrival of the next Ice Age to sweating out the prospect of rapid global warming as the polar ice caps melt. The best any meteorologist can do is remain informed, provide information on climate change, and propose a few ideas about what, if anything, any of us can do about it.

Climate change is a perfectly normal fact of nature. The earth's climate has cycled constantly through warm and cold epochs over hundreds of millions of years and will continue to do so into the future. Careful studies of tree rings, ice cores, and sediment layers all show that our atmosphere has been both substantially warmer and colder than it is today. Our climate is simply the average of all the variety we see in our daily weather. We must admit, however, that climate changes since the Industrial Age have been dramatic. So the question becomes: Are we, the nearly six billion people who populate the earth, hastening the changes in our climate? Thousands of scientists and political leaders worldwide focus on this very question. In fact, when the Intergovernmental Panel on Climate Change (IPCC), an international group involving 2,500 scientists, met in Berlin in 1995, they signed a document stating that "the balance of evidence suggests that there is a discernible human influence on global climate."

When I was studying meteorology at the University of Wisconsin in the mid-1970s, some of the leading authorities on climate change were doing research there. Dr. Reid Bryson, one of the founders of the university's meteorology department, was a frequent lecturer and his specialty was "The New Ice Age." The prevailing argument at that time was that the climate had been

Mount St. Helens erupts in 1980.

cooling since the 1940s, which meant that we were on a path toward colder winters, shorter growing seasons, dramatic changes in rainfall patterns, and the prospect of worldwide food shortages. And what was the cause of this climatological calamity? Air pollution.

According to Bryson's theory, temperature profiles during the twentieth century showed great variability over the previous six decades, but the overall trend was downward for temperatures since World War II. Increased air pollution was partly responsible for the

Dan Birkenheuer: High-Tech Weather Forecasting

While most Coloradans find the state's unpredictable weather frustrating at times, Dan Birkenheuer of Forecast Systems Laboratory (FSL) in Boulder considers our late spring blizzards, violent hailstorms, and sudden tornadoes perfect grist for his mill. Creator of the Local Analysis and Prediction Systems (LAPS) software used by the National Weather Service, Birkenheuer notes that LAPS is particularly useful in Colorado for the very reason that the weather can be so complex. "With our diverse microclimates and hard-to-forecast Front Range, it's a good place for a local-scale model. It might help us figure out where it's going to precipitate more over a small area like Lakewood versus Loveland—it can get down to that resolution."

Birkenheuer, who has a master's degree in meteorology from the South Dakota School of Mines and a doctorate from the University of Denver, has been with FSL for 20 years. During that time, the city of Denver has been a productive guinea pig for working out the bugs of FSL's software. "It's the place where we would take our advanced technologies and share them," he says. "We'd prototype them in Boulder, shake them down, get them more or less bulletproof, take them down to Denver, and let them run in a real forecast environment." The Denver trials have helped FSL develop software that could replace the

National Weather Service's antiquated automated observational systems.

FSL's workstation is probably the most advanced system used anywhere in the United States, according to Birkenheuer. Its primary advantage is that it makes satellite data more accessible to forecast offices "in a way that the forecaster could loop the data into real time." Before the installation of this technology, forecasters were limited in how they could use satellite data, and often, there was no way to match up data with available pictures. Birkenheuer says, "With this system, forecasters can put analysis, data, and forecast vector fields right on top of the imagery and see how they merge up."

FSL's system is currently running at the Denver National Weather Service as the official deployment of the Advanced Weather Interactive Processing System (AWIPS). The AWIPS system is now deployed throughout the United States, and its models are run at the National Center for Environmental Prediction (NCEP) in Washington, D.C. Storm chasers can access FSL's web page to see satellite photographs of upcoming meteorological events, but as Birkenheuer says, the chief aim of the system is to reduce casualties. "Better warnings mean more lead time," he says.

cooling trend because tiny bits of ash, smoke, and dirt (called aerosols) blocked out incoming sunlight and kept some of the sun's energy from reaching the surface of the earth. Given the brutally cold winters of the 1970s, it seemed plausible that we were on the edge of a dangerous precipice.

Volcanoes

The idea of cooling was not far-fetched. In fact, cold snaps happen naturally in this way. When volcanoes erupt, they pour vast amounts of dust and smoke into our atmosphere and the resultant cooling is easy to pick up in worldwide climate surveys. For instance, the eruption of Mount Pinatubo in the Philippines in 1991 resulted in a worldwide cooling of one to two degrees F for about a year and a half before the volcanic aerosols settled out of the atmosphere.

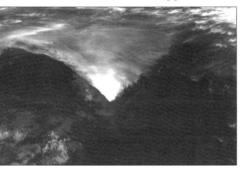

Satellite view of the Mount Pinatubo eruption.

Mount St. Helens ash plume

Other major eruptions have had similar effects on the climate. In August 1883, the Indonesian Island of Krakatoa exploded with the force of many hydrogen bombs. The eruption blew vast clouds of volcanic dust and smoke fifty miles into the atmosphere and totally blocked out the sun for two days within a fifty-mile radius of the island. Global winds swept the volcanic clouds around the world, and sunshine was reduced by ten percent during the next three years. Winters that were colder than average followed the eruption at Krakatoa, as they did after other major volcanic events at Tambora in the East Indies in 1815, Mount Katmai in Alaska in 1912, and Mount Agung on the island of Bali in 1963. In 1980, Mount St. Helens was a dramatic eruption close to home, but the difference was that not much got into the stratosphere, where it does not get rained out—a key point for climate effect.

Considering the effect that volcanic activity has on climate, scientists have come to view industrial pollution as a kind of man-made volcanic ash also cooling the earth. Researchers in the Bryson camp went so far as to theorize that industrialization and its by-products had as much impact on the environment as did natural phenomena. If all the world's cities put out as much particulate matter as a volcano, they claimed, the planet should cool significantly over the 1970s and 1980s.

Nolan Doesken: Ready for Weather in the Twenty-First Century

Although watching the sky for weather changes is an occupation as old as time, Coloradans stand poised at the turn of the century armed with more accessible weather information than ever before. High-tech weather monitoring equipment is a blessing; after all, hasn't Colorado experienced more violent weather recently than in the past?

"If you look at the data, it says yes," replies Nolan Doesken, Assistant State Climatologist at the Colorado Climate Center at Colorado State University (CSU) since 1977. "But that doesn't necessarily mean more dramatic weather is actually occurring. We now have more data and more interest in storm chasing, and I'm convinced that this has created a trend in increased reporting." As an example, Nolan points out that the number of tornadoes reported on the Front Range has increased dramatically—but so has the population, which has created an increased awareness of twisters. In far northeastern Colorado, where growth has not been as significant and people have always been tornado-savvy, the numbers have remained the same.

Yet Doesken admits that increased urbanization has impacted Colorado's climate. In addition to altering the surface vegetation, building new structures, and laying down pavement, "the urban areas in Denver are in some ways replacing dry land with wetter areas, which makes a cooler and more humid climate," Doesken says.

As development spreads west, too, a host of new meteorological concerns take root. "Along the Front Range, we have downslope winds that come and flush pollutants out," Doesken explains. "But in Crested Butte, Steamboat, and Vail, the air will stagnate for weeks. Should western Colorado see large increases in population, air quality will be a larger issue there than it is here along the Front Range."

Whatever the future holds for the state's climate, Doesken favors a decidedly low-tech approach to meteorology. Although he gives flashy automated weather stations their due, in his opinion nothing tops the human touch when it comes to collecting data. Having monitored the weather history of Colorado for over 20 years at CSU, Doesken believes that when it comes to measuring rain or snow, it helps to have a human involved.

Global Warming and Pollution

Ask many scientists today about climate changes, though, and what you'll hear about is global warming. Many people wonder: What is going on with meteorologists? Just a generation ago experts claimed that we were "headed for the new ice age" because of air pollution, and now we are "about to melt the ice caps" because of air pollution!

The reality is that even in the 1970s, some scientists warned that the earth would be warming up. Dr. J. Murray Mitchell, a senior research climatologist with the National Oceanic and Atmospheric Administration (NOAA) who studied the effects of industrial gases, was one of the first to predict a warming trend. And even today, other scientists claim that there has not been a measurable warming of the earth. Noting that temperatures are often reported in large cities, researchers like Fred Singer, professor of environmental sciences at the University of Virginia, argue that cities tend to be considerably warmer than the surrounding countryside because the buildings and blacktop store heat very effectively. Because of the "urban heat island" effect, an artificial warming trend may be reported. Even so, the most recent analysis systems factor in this effect.

Beyond these debates, scientists do agree that cooling and warming trends have different causes. The flip side of industrial and urban pollution from tiny particles or aerosols is the variety of gases that are belched into the atmosphere. When you burn a lump of coal, for instance, you blow not only soot into the atmosphere, but also by-product gases like sulfur dioxide and carbon dioxide. Sulfur emissions react in the atmosphere to form nasty smog conditions, while carbon dioxide is a chief component of the "greenhouse effect."

Denver's brown cloud

The Greenhouse Effect

Far from being a bad thing, the greenhouse effect makes life possible on earth. Without our atmosphere, the average global temperature would be about sixty degrees colder, and the earth would be frozen and lifeless. Our atmosphere traps some of the sun's heat by absorbing the energy and radiating that warmth back to the surface of the earth. The incoming solar energy arrives at the top of our atmosphere with the intensity of thirteen 100-watt lightbulbs over every square yard. About a third of this energy is immediately reflected back into space by dust and clouds. The remaining two-thirds travels down to the earth's surface, where some of it is reflected back to space by water and snow, a little is absorbed directly by the atmosphere, and the rest is absorbed by the earth's surface. The absorbed energy warms the ground and water. That warmth then radiates back into space at a lower temperature than the incoming solar energy. Various gases, water vapor, carbon dioxide, methane, and nitrous oxide act like a blanket by keeping some of this "earth energy" from escaping back into space. This "atmospheric blanket effect" is what we refer to as the greenhouse effect.

The greenhouse effect is not a new concept—the theory was first quantified by a Swedish chemist named Arrhenius in 1896—nor is it unusual in the solar system. Our nearby planetary neighbors also have greenhouse effects. On cold Mars, the atmosphere is weak, so most of the incoming solar energy escapes back into space. Venus's thick atmosphere captures more of

> Far from being a bad thing, the greenhouse effect makes life possible on earth.

THE GREENHOUSE EFFECT

Solar radiation from the sun is absorbed and warms the earth's surface.

This absorbed energy is emitted as infrared radiation from the earth.

Greenhouse gases in Earth's atmosphere absorb some of the escaping infrared radiation and release it back into the atmosphere. This warms the planet and allows life as we know it to exist. Human activities, such as burning fossil fuel and deforestation, have released more greenhouse gases into the atmosphere. This allows more infrared radiation to be absorbed and re-released. This may increase global warming and alter Earth's climate.

the sun's heat, and the result is a surface temperature hot enough to melt lead! Earth, balanced in between, possesses a greenhouse effect that is just about right. Or is it?

For the past 200 years, people have been burning more fossil fuels and pouring amazing amounts of pollutants into the atmosphere. The amount of carbon dioxide in the atmosphere has risen about 25 percent in that time, from about 280 parts per million to 356 parts per million today. Everyday human activity currently releases about seven billion metric tons of carbon dioxide into the air every year, adding to the 750 billion metric tons that are already there. Of that seven billion tons, only about three billion stay in the atmosphere; the rest is absorbed by plants and the oceans. This "carbon sink" capacity complicates the issue of global warming, because the oceans may continue to have a vast holding capacity for carbon dioxide. Plants actually thrive on increased carbon dioxide, and some experts, like Dr. Kenneth Boote, Professor of Agronomy at

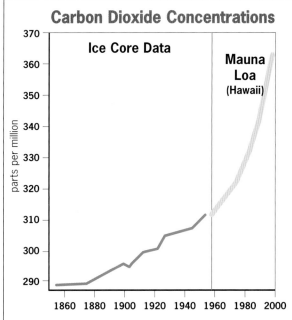

the University of Florida, even claim that the continued release of carbon dioxide will make the earth a much more lush and desirable planet. At the same time, other experts worry that increased carbon dioxide will worsen greenhouse warming and cause more frequent and severe droughts in key agricultural areas.

Many atmospheric scientists today agree that humans have already enhanced global warming. In the 1970s, the quandary was, "Why are we cooling down, when we should be warming up?" The past two decades have seen the cooling trend

reverse dramatically. Although the dust and soot injected into the atmosphere since World War II may have blocked out enough sunlight to cause some cooling in the 1960s and 1970s, scientists now theorize that increased greenhouse gases have produced a warming of the atmosphere. Figures from the President's Office of Science and Technology Policy (OSTP) note that the over the last century, the average surface temperature of the earth has increased by about

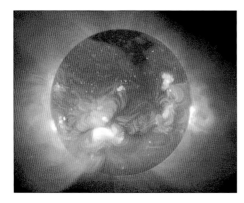

A thermal map of sunspot activity.

Torrential rain caused this flood in Sterling in 1997.

one degree F and that the eleven warmest years this century have all occurred since 1980.

Now, a degree of average warming may not seem like much, but it only took an average degree of cooling to create the "Mini-Ice Age" in Europe from 1570 to 1730. This period of unusual cold created famine in Europe from crop failures and caused glaciers to greatly expand in the Alps. No one knows for sure what the cause was, but the cold may have been related to a great decrease in sunspot activity called the Maunder Minimum. When sunspots are at a low point in their various cycles, the mean output of energy from the sun drops and less heat reaches the earth. What this historical event teaches us is that even a small deviation in average temperature can have far-reaching effects.

Whatever the cause of that event, there are some ominous signs now that the climate is warming. Glaciers are shrinking at an alarming rate. In Alaska, the Columbia Glacier used to tower 200 feet over Prince William Sound, but in the past sixteen years, the glacier has retreated more than eight miles from the sound. Between Valdez and Fairbanks, huge expanses of spruce forest are dead and gray, killed by a population explosion of spruce bark beetles thriving in warmer temperatures. Areas of permafrost in central Alaska are thawing, and forests there are drowning as they sink into the soggy swamp forming beneath them. Scientists at the University of Alaska report that the temperatures in Alaska, Siberia, and northwest Canada have risen an average of five degrees in the past thirty years, with the warming most pronounced in the winter.

Meanwhile, global mean sea level has risen four to ten inches over the past century, mainly because water expands when heated. This rise, if it continues, could be a major source of coastal flooding along the shores of the United States and a catastrophe for many island nations around the world. A warmer climate should produce more severe variations in the precipitation patterns, too. According to the National Climatic Data Center of NOAA, precipitation in the United States has increased by about 6 percent since 1900, while the frequency of intense precipitation events (heavy downpours of more than two inches per day) has increased by 20 percent. This change has caused flooding, soil erosion, drought, and even loss of life.

Rainforest deforestation

So in the words of Stan Laurel, "What do we do now, Ollie?" That is not an easy question to answer. At the International Summit on Climate Change, held in Kyoto, Japan, in December 1997, a treaty was signed by nations around the world. The purpose of this treaty was to create limits on the production of greenhouse gases, chiefly carbon dioxide, to levels produced in 1990. Trying to reach a consensus on this issue is where the science really shifts from the physical to the political. Because the United States is by far the largest producer of greenhouse gases, cutting back on our consumption of fossil fuels would be a bitter pill to swallow. Similarly, developing countries feel that they have a right to exploit their supplies of coal, oil, and forests as developed nations have. Deforestation, a particular problem in the developing world, contributes to greenhouse gases, because wood-burning releases more carbon dioxide and the loss of forests reduces the uptake of carbon dioxide from photosynthesis. Attempting to establish international policies on the reduction of greenhouse gases will be the source of great political debate for years to come.

Scientists hope that the cause could be the cure. Technology may be to blame for the mess, but other advancements in technology have increased the efficiency of our automobiles and industries. Cities are also much cleaner today than they were fifty years ago, even considering population increases. In recent years, we have been able to find some solutions to such major atmospheric problems as acid rain and ozone depletion. Acid rain is an important issue. The emission of sulfurous gases, mainly from power plants, can change the pH of rain and snow, creating conditions that kill plants growing downstream. Recently developed scrubbers can remove the sulfurous gases from power plant smoke.

Acid rain is a concern in Colorado's high country.

The Ozone Layer

A better-known incidence when technology stepped in to repair an environmental disaster centers on the ozone layer. The ozone layer is a thin but vital layer of ozone gas that blocks harmful ultraviolet light; without it, there would be a dramatic rise in skin cancer and a reduction in agricultural yields. In the mid-1970s, two researchers at the University of California at Irvine, Dr. Sherwood

Twin Troublemakers: El Niño and La Niña
An Interview with Kevin Trenberth and Michael Glantz

Kevin Trenberth

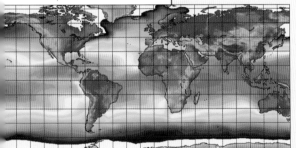

Satellite measurements of ocean temperatures during an El Niño event.

The first time most Coloradans took El Niño seriously was in 1997, when the much-maligned warming pattern was blamed for everything from violent weather to plane delays to higher produce prices at the super-market. But for Kevin Trenberth and Michael Glantz, senior scientists at the National Center for Atmospheric Research (NCAR) in Boulder, El Niño and its sister-phenomenon La Niña are simply recently known and little-documented facts of the earth's climate.

As Trenberth explains, El Niño patterns last usually one to two years and occur every three to five years. During a period of El Niño activity, warmer waters in the Pacific Ocean heat the atmosphere, causing world temperatures to climb as much as 0.5 degree F and generating climate problems worldwide. El Niño was first named in the nineteenth century when the Peruvian fish harvest was affected by the warming of the ocean. The United States took notice of El Niño in the 1970s, when a sharp reduction in the Pacific anchovy catches affected American poultry farms where anchovy fishmeal is used in chicken feed, and anchovy prices increased. El Niño naturally alternates with cooler La Niña. The most recent La Niña began in late spring 1998 and brought cooler and wetter conditions to the Pacific Northwest and northern states, but milder and drier-than-normal conditions to the southern states from Southern California to Florida in the 1998–1999 winter.

Since the mid-1970s, scientists have tracked El Niño patterns eight times but La Niñas only four times. Does the frequency of the warmer, drier pattern reflect a generalized warming of the planet? "That's the $64,000 question," says Trenberth, who heads up the Climate Analysis Section at NCAR. "We've seen more El Niños than we expected. I personally think there is an influence of global warming on El Niño." According to Trenberth, global warming may mean more El Niños.

Glantz, the author of the first popular overview of El Niño, *Currents of Change* (1996), is a little more cautious. Pointing out that computer models are not yet really good at forecasting El Niño events several months in advance, Glantz says that studying the effect of global warming on El Niño is simply going to take more time.

Even so, Trenberth and Glantz agree that "global warming is showing its face." Whether El Niño and La Niña are increasing in frequency or scientists are just noticing them more, these weather patterns can serve as an important key to the improved understanding of a potentially threatening change in the earth's climate. "We're beginning to see the signs of global warming," Trenberth says. "We should heed the signs."

Susan Solomon: Clearing the Air About Ozone Depletion

The first thing that Dr. Susan Solomon wants you to know about ozone depletion is that it does not cause global warming. Confusing one for the other is a common mistake, but actually the two climatological problems are vastly unalike. A senior scientist at the Aeronomy Laboratory at the National Oceanic and Atmospheric Administration (NOAA) in Boulder, Solomon explains that while ozone depletion does increase the earth's exposure to ultraviolet light, the main source of heat on the earth's surface is visible light. The earth cools itself mainly by giving off infrared light. Therefore, global warming is caused when carbon dioxide builds up in the atmosphere and "absorbs the infrared light, and the atmosphere heats up like a blanket," she says.

Ozone depletion poses its own set of problems for the environment. As Solomon

notes above, ozone acts as a shield against ultraviolet radiation; left to its own devices, the ozone layer in the stratosphere reaches a natural equilibrium. When scientists first discovered the hole in the ozone layer in the mid-1980s, it was a project headed up by Solomon and other scientists that obtained the first evidence that inert chlorofluorocarbons (CFCs), found in refrigerants, solvents, and aerosols, were responsible for the damage. As Solomon

(Below) Satellite measurements show ozone depletion from October 1979 to October 1987.

explains, "CFCs have a long residence time, and they are unusual in that they are extremely inert. They don't react with water molecules and are not water-soluble. This means they don't rain out. The only place for them to go is up into the stratosphere. That's why this is a global and not just a regional problem."

CFCs are no longer produced in this country (the United States was one of 70 nations that agreed in 1987 to stop production of CFCs by the end of the century), but we all must live with the consequences. Especially in Colorado, where high altitudes make those effects more acute, people should educate themselves about the ramifications of ozone depletion. In Boulder, for example, where they have been measuring ozone levels since the 1960s, there is up to 8% less ozone in the atmosphere than there was 20 years ago. "This gives you a 10% to 20% increase in potential for skin cancer," Solomon says, noting that the worst ozone depletion is in winter and spring. Coloradans now have even more reason to wear sunscreen when they ski.

On a practical level, Coloradans can recycle older appliances that contain CFCs (most communities in Colorado have such facilities—the Yellow Pages will list them). Be aware, however, that ameliorating the damage is simply going to take time. As Solomon states, "What's destroying ozone is man-made, and it's going to take at least 50 years to get rid of it."

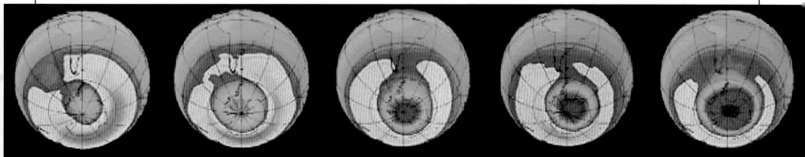

Rowland and Dr. Mario Molina, discovered that the ozone layer was being destroyed by chemicals called chlorofluorocarbons (CFCs), especially around the South Pole. These chemicals were thought to be inert and harmless, but in fact, they would interact with other chemicals high in the stratosphere and destroy ozone molecules. The Nobel Prize-winning research of Sherwood and Molina led to the Montreal Protocol Agreement in 1987, which called for a dramatic reduction in the use of CFCs worldwide. Despite the importance of CFCs in the manufacture of air conditioners, cleaners for electronics, and aerosol propellants, the alarming loss of ozone prompted industries to find safe alternatives to CFCs. In the decade since the Montreal Protocol was signed, CFC pollution has dropped substantially, and the thinning of the ozone layer has slowed down.

Alternatives and Solutions

So the challenge that faces us in the years ahead will be two-fold. First, it behooves all of us to increase our "environ-mentality." In other words, learn as much as you can about environmental issues that face Colorado, the United States, and the world. Educate yourself so that you can ask questions and challenge political leaders on these issues. Because environmental issues can be so politically charged, be wary of what you read. Try to discern the motive of the authors you are reading; in other words, find out who is paying them and ask whether they have a certain agenda. Take note if an author claims that we shouldn't worry about mankind's influence on the environment, but works for an industry with a poor environmental track record. Similarly, watch out for doomsday prophecies from some researcher whose motivation may be affected by a need for a greater supply of grant money.

The actions we take in the coming years will determine the legacy we leave to future generations.

Be a modest consumer. We all can put into practice what we already know: reduce, reuse, and recycle. Reducing the miles you drive, turning the lights off, and monitoring the level of your thermostat are all things you can do to decrease the amount of greenhouse gases in the air. Reusing and recycling cut down on the consumption of fossil fuels and lessen the need for landfill space.

Support clean technologies, both politically and with your pocketbook. You can do this through Public Service Company's WindSource program. By spending just a few pennies more per kilowatt on your monthly bill, you can ensure that wind-generating power stations around Colorado are developed. The energy that

powers the weather computers, lights, and cameras in the 9NEWS Weather Center comes from a Public Service Company wind farm north of Fort Collins. Likewise, in Denver, the National Center for Renewable Energy is working on other clean technologies, like photovoltaic cells that produce electricity directly from sunlight. They are cheaper, longer-lasting, and more energy-efficient.

Another example of cleaner energy is the Department of Energy's (DOE) program to promote biomass fuel production. This renewable fuel uses certain crops to produce methane fuel, often from previously discarded agricultural by-products. This technology is currently operating at two demonstration sites, one in Vermont and the other in Hawaii. The DOE is also developing clean geothermal energy. Using the heat of the earth, steam can be produced to run electrical turbines and heat water for heating systems in buildings. This technology can only be used in areas where geothermal heat is close to the surface, but it produces no greenhouse gases.

Another source of clean energy, nuclear energy, has gotten a bad reputation because of accidents at Three Mile Island and Chernobyl. While we should be cautious in using nuclear fission, nuclear fusion is another matter. With fission, the splitting of large atoms of uranium creates tremendous problems with nuclear waste. With fusion, two hydrogen atoms are combined and create helium, in the same way the sun produces energy. Because hydrogen is the most common element in the universe, the power supply using fusion would be limitless. So far, we only know how to create fusion through the explosion of a hydrogen bomb! Obviously, more research is needed before we can harness the "power of the sun," but you can support funding for fusion research.

Nuclear fusion, wind power, geothermal energy, and photo-voltaic cells may eventually replace fossil fuels as our primary energy sources. Until then, support research on climate change and use fossil fuel resources more efficiently. The actions we take in the coming years will determine the legacy we leave to future generations. Ultimately, we should heed the words of Thomas Jefferson, who wrote in 1789, "I say the earth belongs to each . . . generation during its course, fully and in its own right, [and] no generation can contract debts greater than may be paid during the course of its own existence."

Ed Greene: An Expert at Explaining the Weather

Ed Greene likes to take his weather show on the road. A fixture on the Denver meteorology scene since his first job as a forecaster in 1976, Greene devotes much of his spare time explaining the weather to community groups and school kids. He received his first request to talk to a school about weather—a group of third graders at Niwot Elementary School—17 years ago, and he's gone back every year since.

Like many weathercasters, Ed Greene became interested in the weather as a child. Growing up on Long Island, New York, Greene experienced snowstorms, endured heat waves, and saw something Coloradans consider exotic: hurricanes. Although he studied weather at Monmouth College in Illinois, he dreamed of being a rock and roll disc jockey. After graduation in 1972, he went in pursuit of the perfect DJ job. In fact, he was working at a radio station when he was offered his first chance to do television weathercasting.

When he started reporting the weather, Greene says, the only question on the mind of the station manager was, "How can you explain the weather to people and make it enjoyable so that they understand it?" To make learning about weather more fun, Greene offers the following trivia quiz. How much do you know about weather in Colorado?

Ed Greene's Favorite Weather Trivia Questions
Baby, It's Cold Outside

1. What are the highest and lowest temperatures ever recorded in Denver?

2. The longest subzero period in Denver's history was in 1983. For how many days did the mercury stay below zero?

3. Seven U.S. states have recorded temperatures of –60 degrees F or colder. Colorado is one of them—can you name the other six?

It Never Rains but It Pours

4. Which Colorado city endured the state's worst flood on record?

5. On May 22, 1876, the most precipitation to fall in Denver in one calendar day was measured. How many inches of rain fell?

6. On May 12, 1982, northeast Colorado was hit with 3.5 inches of rain. On the same day, how many inches of snow did Coal Creek Canyon get?

If You Can't Take the Heat . . .

7. What is the highest LOW temperature recorded in Denver?

8. The longest stretch of intense heat in Denver happened way back in 1874. For how many days did the high temperature stay above 95 degrees F?

9. A record string of 100-degree days occurred in July 1989 in Denver. For how many days in a row did the heat wave last?

10. What is the record for consecutive days of 100-degree or better days in Grand Junction?

Let It Snow, Let It Snow, Let It Snow

11. Nearly 75% of the time, snow is forecasted for Halloween in Denver. What is the largest amount of snow to fall on trick-or-treaters in the city?

12. During Denver's heaviest five-day snowfall in December 1913, how many inches of snow clogged the city streets?

13. The heaviest official one-day snow amount in Denver history fell on Christmas Eve, 1982. How many inches piled up?

14. The record for the greatest 24-hour snowfall for the western United States was set on April 14–15, 1921, at Silver Lake. How many inches of snow fell on that one day?

15. The average snowfall for Denver in October is a mere 3.7 inches. But in October 1997, how many inches of snow fell to skew that statistic?

For Experts Only

16. When was the latest first snow in Denver and the earliest first snow in Denver?

17. The costliest hailstorm in U.S. history hit the Front Range on July 11, 1990. What was the total damage in dollars?

18. On average, how many tornadoes hit Colorado annually?

19. On average for Denver, which month has the most sunshine and which month has the least?

20. In over 125 years of record keeping, how often has thunder been reported in Denver during the month of February?

Appendix A: Weather Web Sites

For more information on local and national weather, look up these web sites on the Internet:

9NEWS Weather

http://www.9News.com

Features weather forecasts for Colorado and the Denver area. Local radar from Super Doppler 9. Various "LIVE ON" camera views from around Colorado.

The Metropolitan State College of Denver, Department of Earth and Atmospheric Sciences

http://clem.mscd.edu/~eas/

Features local as well as national weather information and current readings gathered from various weather instruments. Offers good links to other weather web sites.

National Weather Service, Denver, Colorado

http://www.crh.noaa.gov/den/

Excellent source for weather information for any Colorado city. Various pages connect you to current reports on weather and forecasts. Includes pages on climatology, current pressure data, NOAA weather radio, monthly data summaries, and others.

gopher://weather.colorado.edu:861/1

Climatic summary for major metro areas in Colorado, including ski reports, avalanche warnings, current forecasts, and road conditions.

http://twister.sbs.ohio-state.edu/colorado.html

Colorado area climate information, observations, hydrometeorology, data, forecasts, and more.

Climate Diagnostic Center (NOAA-CIRES)
National Oceanic and Atmospheric Administration (NOAA)
Cooperative Institute for Research in Environmental Sciences (CIRES)

http://www.cdc.noaa.gov

Focuses on understanding and predicting important climate variations in time.

Mesoscale and Microscale Meteorology National Center for Atmospheric Research

http://www.mmm.ucar.edu/mmm/home.html

Offers weather research, general information, and various other related links.

http://weather.unisys.com/ngm/index/html

Offers hurricane data, weather by the region, 48-hour forecast maps, and the latest observations on a national Zip Code basis.

Pauxsutawney Phil's home page

http://www.groundhog.org/

Provides various information on groundhog day, including past predictions, general information, and the history of groundhog day.

Appendix B: Bibliography

Anderson, Bette Roda. *Weather in the West.* Palo Alto, CA: American West Publishing, 1975.

Boote, Kenneth. *The Greening of Planet Earth.* The Institute for Biosphere Research, Inc. Videotape.

Branley, Franklyn M. *It's Raining Cats and Dogs.* Boston: Houghton Mifflin, 1987.

Bryson, Reid A., and Thomas J. Murray. *Climates of Hunger.* Wisconsin: Univ. of Wisconsin Press, 1977.

Dickinson, Terence. *Exploring the Sky by Day.* Ontario, Canada: Camden House, 1988.

Facklam, Howard, and Margery Facklam. *Changes in the Wind: Earth's Shifting Climate.* San Diego, CA: Harcourt Brace Jovanovich, 1986.

Glantz, Michael H. *Currents of Change.* Cambridge: Cambridge University Press, 1996.

Hensen, Robert. *Television Weathercasting: A History.* Jefferson, NC: McFarland & Company, Inc., 1990.

Keen, Richard A. *SkyWatch: The Western Weather Guide.* Golden, CO: Fulcrum, Inc., 1987.

Kerr, Richard. "Greenhouse Forecasting Still Cloudy." *Science Magazine,* May 1997, pp. 1040–1042.

Kessler, Edwin, Ed. *The Thunderstorm in Human Affairs.* Norman: University of Oklahoma Press, 1983.

Ponte, Lowell. *The Cooling.* Englewood Cliffs, NJ: Prentice Hall, Inc., 1976.

Schneider, Stephen H. *Global Warming.* New York: Vintage Books, 1989.

Singer, Fred S. *The Scientific Case Against the Global Climate Treaty.* The Science and Environmental Policy Project. Fairfax, VA, 1997.

Wilson, Francis. *The Weather Pop-Up Book.* New York: Simon & Schuster, Inc., 1987.

Appendix C: Related Reading

Fields, Alan. *Partly Sunny: The Weather Junkie's Guide to Outsmarting the Weather.* Boulder, CO: Windsor Peak Press, 1995.

Foggitt, Bill. *Weatherwise: Facts, Fictions and Predictions.* Philadelphia, PA: Running Press, 1992.

Forrester, Frank H. *1001 Questions Answered About the Weather.* New York: Dover Publications, 1981.

Glantz, Michael H. *Currents of Change: El Niño's Impact on Climate and Society.* Cambridge: Cambridge University Press, 1996.

Global Climate Change: An East Room Roundtable. Washington, D.C.: Office of Science and Technology Policy, July 1997.

"Greenhouse Wars: Why the Rebels Have a Cause." *New Scientist Magazine,* 19 July 1997.

Greenler, Robert. *Rainbows, Halos, and Glories.* Cambridge: Cambridge Universtiy Press, 1980.

Kerr, Richard. "Among Global Thermometers, Warming Still Wins Out." *Science Magazine,* vol. 281, 25 September 1998.

Lehr, Paul E., R. Will Burnett, and Herbert S. Zim. *Golden Guide to Weather.* New York: Golden Press, 1975.

Ludlum, David M. *National Audubon Society Field Guide to North American Weather.* New York: Chanticleer Press, Inc., 1997.

Schaefer, Vincent J., and John A. Day. *Atmosphere: Clouds, Rain, Snow, Storms.* New York: Houghton Mifflin Co., 1981.

Trenberth, Kevin. "The Use and Abuse of Climate Models." *Nature Magazine,* vol. 386, 13 March 1997.

Trenberth, Kevin E. "What Is Happening to El Niño?" *Encyclopedia Britannica,* Yearbook of Science and the Future, 1997.

Photo Credits

Front Cover: John Fielder (full page); Kevin Graham (top right); John Weaver, NOAA (middle right); NOAA (bottom right)

Inside Front Flap: NCAR

P. 1: Bill Bonebrake (top); Jacque Sykes (middle); Tim Samaras (bottom)

P. 2: Kevin Graham

P. 3: Tim Samaras (top); Ann B. Rutledge (middle); Bill Bonebrake (bottom)

P. 4: The last line in the acknowledgments refers to a James Taylor song, "The Secret of Life"

P. 5: Andy Schaeffer, 9NEWS

P. 6: John Fielder

P. 7: NOAA

P. 8: Kevin Graham (top); Jonathan Moreno (illus.); NCDC (bottom)

P. 9: Craig Keyzer; Jonathan Moreno (illus.)

P. 10: Peter Link (top); Terry Oltragge (middle); Winter Park Resort (bottom)

P. 11: Mike Nelson; Jonathan Moreno (illus.)

P. 12: Tim Samaras; Jonathan Moreno (illus.); data from Robert Glancy, NWS, Denver

P. 13: NCAR; data from Robert Glancy, NWS, Denver

P. 14: NCAR (top); Kevin Graham (bottom left); Bill Bonebrake (bottom right)

P. 15: Brian Litz (top); Bill Bonebrake (middle); Brian Litz (bottom)

P. 16: John Fielder

P. 17: Tim Samaras

P. 18: Peter Link (top four); Kevin Graham (bottom)

P. 19: Peter Link; Jonathan Moreno (illus.)

P. 20: Peter Link (top); Tim Samaras (bottom)

P. 21: NOAA (top and bottom)

P. 22: Andy Schaeffer, 9NEWS; NOAA (top right)

P. 23: Andy Schaeffer, 9NEWS

P. 24: Tim Samaras (top); NOAA (bottom)

P. 25: Jonathan Moreno (illus.)

P. 26: Mike Nelson (top); NOAA (middle); Tim Samaras (bottom)

P. 27: NSSL (top); NOAA (bottom)

P. 28: Jonathan Moreno (illus.); Peter Link

P. 29: NOAA (top); Andy Schaeffer, 9NEWS (bottom)

P. 30: USGS

P. 31: John Weaver, NOAA (top); USFS (bottom)

P. 32: USFS (both at top); Echo Canyon River Expeditions

P. 33: Brian Litz (top left); Bill Bonebrake (top right); Peter Link (bottom)

P. 34: John Fielder

P. 35: Bill Bonebrake

P. 36: Jonathan Moreno (illus.)

P. 37: Kevin Graham (top); Brian Litz (bottom)

P. 38: Bill Bonebrake (top); Kevin Graham (middle); NCAR (bottom)

P. 39: NOAA (top); Jonathan Moreno (illus.)

P. 40: John Dawson

P. 41: Brian Litz (top); Bill Bonebrake (bottom)

P. 42: USFS (both)

P. 43: NOAA (top); Craig Keyzer (middle); John Morrey (bottom)

P. 44: John Fielder

P. 45: Bill Bonebrake

P. 46: NCAR (top); Brian Litz (bottom)

P. 47: Sport Obermeyer (both)

P. 48: Brian Litz (top); Jonathan Moreno (illus.)

P. 49: NCAR; Jonathan Moreno (illus.)

P. 50: NCAR (top); Don Preston (bottom)

P. 51: Brian Litz (top left and right); Bill Bonebrake (bottom left and right)

P. 52: Richard Armstrong, Colorado Geological Survey (all)

P. 53: Richard Armstrong, Colorado Geological Survey (top); Brian Litz (middle)

P. 54: Colorado Avalanche Information Center (top and map); Colorado Historical Society (middle)

P. 55: Brian Litz (top); Peter Link (middle); Ruth Montgomery (bottom)

P. 56: Clockwise from top left: Colorado Historical Society; Carol Silberg, NOAA; Denver Public Library, Western History Dept.; NOAA; Denver Public Library, Western History Dept.

P. 57: NCAR (top); Denver Public Library, Western History Dept. (bottom)

P. 58: Paul Idleman, Old Colorado City History Center (top); Denver Public Library, Western History Dept. (bottom)

P. 59: Ian Paton (top right); Baynaird McNcil (middle and bottom right); Winter Park Ski Resort (bottom left)

P. 60: Nolan Doesken (both)

P. 61: John Weaver, NOAA (top); Denver Public Library, Western History Dept. (bottom)

P. 62: Colorado Historical Society (both)

P. 63: Colorado Historical Society (top); Denver Public Library, Western History Dept. (middle and bottom)

P. 64: Colorado Historical Society (top); Denver Public Library, Western History Dept. (bottom)

P. 65: USGS (both)

P. 66: USGS (top); Jonathan Moreno (illus.)

P. 67: USGS (both)

P. 68: NOAA (top); John Weaver, NOAA (bottom)

P. 69: John Weaver, NOAA (top); Fort Collins Museum (middle); South Platte Sentinel (bottom)

P. 70: Denver Public Library, Western History Dept. (top); USFS (middle); Colorado Historical Society (bottom)

P. 71: Denver Public Library, Western History Dept. (top); South Platte Sentinel (second from top); Colorado Historical Society (third from top); Denver Public Library, Western History Dept. (bottom)

P. 72: Clockwise from top left: Diana Curran; NOAA; Tim Samaras; Peter Link; NOAA

P. 73: Tim Samaras

P. 74: Eric Kehe (all)

P. 75: Tim Samaras (top and bottom); NOAA (middle)

P. 76: Donald Burkhart; Jonathan Moreno (illus.)

P. 77: NOAA (top); Harlan E. Lindberg (bottom)

P. 78: Jonathan Moreno (illus.)

P. 79: Tim Samaras (top); William D. Platt (bottom)

P. 80: Tim Samaras (all)

P. 81: Tim Samaras (both)

P. 82: Tim Samaras (top); NOAA (middle); NCAR (bottom)

P. 83: NOAA (both)

P. 84: NOAA; Jonathan Moreno (illus.)

P. 85: NOAA; Musser Moore (bottom)

P. 86: John Laughlin (top); Tim Samaras (bottom)

P. 87: NOAA (top); Tim Samaras (bottom)

P. 88: Andy Schaeffer, 9NEWS (left); Mike Nelson (top and middle right); NOAA (bottom right)

P. 89: Mike Nelson (top); Terry Elkins (bottom)

P. 90: NOAA (top and bottom)

P. 91: Terry Kelly (top); Mike Nelson (bottom)

P. 92: Mike Nelson (top); Andy Schaeffer, 9NEWS (bottom)

P. 93: Jonathan Moreno (illus.)

P. 94: Mike Nelson (all)

P. 95: Mike Nelson (top); Thomas Christopher Moore (bottom)

P. 96: Kevin Graham (top); Andy Schaeffer, 9NEWS (bottom)

P. 97: Mike Nelson (top); NOAA (bottom)

P. 98: NOAA (both)

P. 99: Peter Link (top); Jonathan Moreno (illus.)

P. 100: NOAA (top); Tim Samaras (bottom)

P. 101: NOAA

P. 102: Peter Link (top); Andy Schaeffer, 9NEWS (bottom)

P. 103: Maryann Adams (top); Andy Schaeffer, 9NEWS (bottom)

P. 104: Peter Link (top); Andy Schaeffer, 9NEWS (bottom)

P. 105: Ruth Montgomery (top); Sharon Koch (bottom)

P. 106: John Fielder (all but lower left); NOAA (lower left)

P. 107: John Fielder (all)

P. 108: John Fielder (top); Carl Swanson, III (middle); NOAA (bottom)

P. 109: John Fielder

P. 110: Sylvia Lujan (top left); Ronald D. Coil (top right); Jack Weust (middle left); Dewayne Fenton (middle right); W. Gordon Copley (bottom)

P. 111: Andrea Ferency (top left); Terry Williford (top right); Marie D. Lawson (middle left); Nancy Schara (middle right); Bonnie N. Handy (bottom)

P. 112: Ken Stevenson (top); William D. Platt (top right); Mark Knox (middle); Helen D. Lambert (bottom left); Barbara A. Larson (bottom right)

P. 113: George E. Chenoweth (top); Charles J. Gadway (middle); Jay Gustafson (bottom); Jonathan Moreno (illus.)

P. 114: Eric Kehe (all)

P. 115: NOAA

P. 116: NASA (large Earth photo); NCAR (top right); NOAA (middle left); NASA (bottom left)

P. 117: NOAA (top); USGS, Cascades Volcano Observatory (bottom)

P. 118: NOAA (top); John Laughlin (bottom)

P. 119: NOAA; USGS, Cascades Volcano Observatory

P. 120: NCAR (top); John Laughlin (bottom)

P. 121: NCAR (top); Brian Litz (bottom)

P. 122: Bill Bonebrake (top); Jonathan Moreno (illus.)

P. 123: Mike Nelson

P. 124: NASA (top); NCAR (middle); South Platte Sentinel (bottom)

P. 125: NCAR (top); Brian Litz (bottom)

P. 126: John Laughlin; NASA (illus.)

P. 127: Susan Solomon (both); NASA (illus.)

P. 128: Brian Litz (all except bottom left); Public Service Company (bottom left)

P. 129: Brian Litz

P. 130: Andy Schaeffer, 9NEWS (top); Bill Bonebrake (bottom right); Peter Link (bottom left)

P. 131: Lynn Whalin (top); Tim Samaras (bottom)

P. 132: Kevin Graham

P. 133: Tim Samaras

P. 134: Mark Knox

P. 135: Kevin Graham

P. 136: Andy Schaeffer, 9NEWS

Inside Back Flap: Andy Schaeffer, 9NEWS

Back Cover: NCAR (both)

ABBREVIATIONS
NASA: National Aeronautics and Space Administration
NCAR: National Center for Atmospheric Research
NCDC: National Climatic Data Center
NOAA: National Oceanic and Atmospheric Administration
NSSL: National Severe Storm Laboratory
NWS: National Weather Service
USFS: U.S. Forest Service
USGS: U.S. Geological Survey

Note: Most photographs in this book were taken in Colorado; the exceptions show specific weather conditions.

Index

Entries in bold denote pages with illustrations or photographs.

9NEWS

Colorado's Weather Leaders

Mike Nelson

Mike Nelson began his weather career over twenty years ago, and came to Denver in 1991. He is a eight-time winner of the regional Emmy award for Best Weathercaster, and helped develop the computerized Weather Central Graphics System used by over 500 television stations around the world. Mike has served on the Broadcast Board of the American Meteorological Society.

Mike appears on 9NEWS at 5:00 P.M., 6:00 P.M., and 10:00 P.M. and can be heard on KHOW and KOA radio.

Nick Carter

Nick Carter has prepared weather forecasts in Illinois, in Louisiana as the chief meteorologist, and here in Colorado since 1984. He became a meteorologist in 1982 and has his AMS Seal of Approval. Nick is a licensed commercial pilot, and is also a part-time instructor of meteorology at Metropolitan State College in Denver.

Nick appears on 9NEWS at noon and on weekend mornings.

Ed Greene

Ed Greene has been predicting weather in Denver for many years, and joined 9NEWS in 1996. Originally from Long Island, New York, Ed began his career in radio but found his true calling when he began forecasting weather on television.

Ed Greene appears on 9NEWS at Daybreak at 5:00 A.M., and at 6:00 A.M. and 4:00 P.M. Ed's weather reports can also be heard on KOA radio, 850AM, during morning and evening drive hours.

Kathy Sabine

Kathy joined the 9NEWS weather team in 1993. She brought to 9NEWS her experience in weather and general assignment reporting from television stations in San Luis Obispo, Santa Barbara, Salinas, and San Jose, California. Kathy produces *The More You Know* segments with stories about interesting and innovative programs in education.

Kathy appears on the 9NEWS weekend edition and at noon on weekdays.